COOK JAPAN

STAY SLIM • LIVE LONGER

COOK JAPAN
STAY SLIM • LIVE LONGER

Reiko Hashimoto

Absolute Press
An imprint of Bloomsbury Publishing Plc

50 Bedford Square
London
WC1B 3DP
UK

1385 Broadway
New York
NY 10018
USA

www.bloomsbury.com

ABSOLUTE PRESS and the A. logo are trademarks of Bloomsbury Publishing Plc

First published 2017

© Reiko Hashimoto, 2017
Photography © Jodi Hinds, 2017

Reiko Hashimoto has asserted her right under the Copyright, Designs and Patents Act, 1988, to be identified as Author of this work.

British Library Cataloguing-in-Publication Data
A catalogue record for this book is available from the British Library.

Library of Congress Cataloguing-in-Publication data has been applied for.

ISBN: HB: 978-1-4729-3323-2
ePDF: 978-1-4729-3325-6
ePub: 978-1-4729-3324-9

2 4 6 8 10 9 7 5 3 1

Printed and bound in China by C&C Offset

Bloomsbury Publishing Plc makes every effort to ensure that the papers used in the manufacture of our books are natural, recyclable products made from wood grown in well-managed forests. Our manufacturing processes conform to the environmental regulations of the country of origin.

To find out more about our authors and books visit www.bloomsbury.com. Here you will find extracts, author interviews, details of forthcoming events and the option to sign up for our newsletters.

CONTENTS

6   Preface

7   Introduction

13   Equipment and Utensils

17   Storecupboard Ingredients

21   Fresh Ingredients

24   Drinks

27   Basics and Sauces

33   Small Bites

51   Rice

71   Noodles

93   Fish and Shellfish

115   Meat and Poultry

137   Vegetables and Seaweed

159   Tofu and Egg

181   Nabe

193   Sushi

209   Sweet

231   Index

239   Acknowledgements and About the Author

PREFACE

Seventeen years ago I moved to London from Japan and after three years I began my cookery school, Hashi Cooking. I teach students – ranging from complete beginners to professional chefs – how to make authentic Japanese recipes, with a little fusion inspired by my travels around the world.

I had never dreamt that my teaching could reach the level that it is now, but it seemed to develop naturally. I enjoy interacting and connecting with people. It's always been in me. Teaching my culinary heritage and Japanese cooking skills is an extremely important part of my life and I feel extremely blessed to do what I am most passionate about.

Growing up, I was fortunate enough to have had a mother who cooked fresh food for each and every meal, every day. I remember, as a child, I would wake up and go downstairs to the familiar sound of grating in the kitchen. This was my mother, shaving a solid piece of dried and smoked bonito fish to make the flakes for dashi stock. Each day she would shave the fish to obtain the freshest bonito flakes that were then made into dashi stock for miso soup, which was served at breakfast. These days most home cooks use instant dashi stock powder to make this soup, but if you were brought up with the fresh, real flavour it is hard to come to terms with these fast, modern alternatives.

My family continue to live in Kyoto where I grew up, a city in which we always had an abundance of seasonal mountain vegetables. Like most Japanese chefs, I learnt to cook with the seasons to achieve the best flavours. I return to Japan once a year, often in the spring or autumn as this is when my favourite ingredients are available. Early in the spring, I look out for the woody and nutty flavour of freshly picked bamboo shoots, while in autumn I am drawn towards *matsutake* mushrooms, also known as the Japanese truffle. Simmered lightly in dashi stock and served with the citrus fruit yuzu to cut through their earthy flavour, these mushrooms taste divine.

It is these moments of sheer joy that have developed my dedication to real Japanese flavours, and to introduce them to others through my teaching. At its core, my teaching style looks to challenge the myth that Japanese cooking is complex and mysterious. I want to break down these barriers by providing easy-to-follow recipes and cooking methods that can be painlessly adapted to the Western kitchen, as well as explaining the versatility and nutritional properties of unfamiliar ingredients.

The Japanese Diet

As a health-conscious chef, I have long been aware of the specific health benefits of the Japanese diet. Japan boasts one of the highest life expectancies in the world, and only 3.6 per cent of the Japanese population have a body mass index over 30, which is the international standard for obesity, compared to 32 per cent of Americans. The reasons for this are undoubtedly the diet, with many Japanese people subscribing to the notion 'eat with your eyes' – a nod to the importance of colours, crockery and food presentation.

Typically, Japanese meals consist of an array of textures and flavours, which are eaten slowly and, in comparison to the western diet, contain fewer fats or processed ingredients, and far less dairy and meat. Versatile ingredients such as miso and two of my personal favourites – seaweed and tofu – contain an array of vitamins and minerals that promote excellent health, and most importantly lead to mouthwateringly good food. Tofu is revered in Japan, and Kyoto in particular is famous for the delicacy of its tofu, but in the west this ingredient is often neglected or considered vegetarian-only. Tofu is something I try to eat every day during my visits to Kyoto, as it is beautifully clean and rich and you can find a huge variety of types from different regions. I suppose we see tofu as the French see cheese. Although it may be unlikely to find tofu of quite the same quality in the UK, the recipes in this book, I hope, will teach an appreciation of this unique and delicious ingredient.

Offering authentic and clearly explained recipes, this book is your gateway to the cuisine that gives Japan one of the lowest obesity rates and longest life expectancies in the world. It also offers you an insight into the food culture of Japan, which has remained so close to my heart.

INTRODUCTION

COOK JAPAN

Food really is central to Japanese culture. From mothers creating bento boxes each day for their children to take to school to friends gathering around a *nabemono* (hotpot) for a shared meal or visiting sushi bars to have your food prepared in front of your eyes – food is everywhere.

In Japan we have different kinds of restaurants for different kinds of foods and experiences and visit them accordingly: an *okonomi-yaki* restaurant for an *okonomi-yaki* pancake, a ramen shop for ramen noodles (and each with its own speciality broth), and of course a sushi bar for sushi. Japanese diners have an extremely discerning palate, especially when it comes to rice. In fact, many people might be surprised to hear that sushi restaurants are rated based on the quality of their rice rather than their fish.

Another crucial aspect of Japanese food, especially sushi, is presentation, something which has made the dish popular worldwide. The importance of presentation is key to every meal every day in Japan, as families dine from many small and beautiful pieces of crockery, each with its own shape and texture to enhance the appearance of the food and the pleasure of dining. If you ever wondered why Japanese knives are renowned for being so sharp, just consider the visual effect of a perfectly cut piece of fish or vegetable upon a plate. This is why it is crucial to invest in a good knife when beginning your journey into Japanese food. When presenting a meal, consider how you slice your vegetables, tofu or meat and the colour combinations. Bear in mind that when we eat with chopsticks, we tend to slow down so this is another reason why we should try to ensure good presentation. You'll find yourself enjoying looking at your meal for so much longer.

STAY SLIM

Each time I return to Japan I notice that, in general, people are very slim. In recent years the obesity rate in Japan has risen slightly however, coinciding with the increasing popularity of western recipes, food products and eating habits in Japan. So what is it about the traditional Japanese diet that keeps the Japanese so slim?

Typically, Japanese meals consist of an array of dishes, textures and flavours which are eaten slowly with chopsticks, served in small portions and savoured. The Japanese table is considered a work of art, with presentation an extremely important part of the dining experience. This, along with the well-known saying 'eat only until you're 80 per cent full' and the specific set of ingredients we use, have led to Japan having the lowest obesity rate in the developing world.

In comparison to many western diets, the Japanese diet is low in fat – animal fats and dairy in particular – with milk often supplemented with a soy alternative and meat replaced by soya products such as tofu. Tofu is an incredibly versatile ingredient that is so often misused, however it is incredibly high in protein, easy to transform into a delicious dish and contains less fat and fewer calories than the same quantity of meat. The Japanese diet takes the rest of its protein mainly from seeds and fish, the latter of which also contains good fats and minerals.

Although the Japanese diet is low in fat, unlike most modern 'diets' it is not low in starchy carbohydrates, with rice a staple and often eaten at breakfast, lunch and dinner. In fact about half of what a Japanese person eats a day consists of carbohydrates, with fat eaten the least of all. As many nutritionists now explain, carbohydrates are not the cause of weight gain, rather sugar, refined foods and simply over-eating – which is quite difficult to do when one is eating such a range of flavours and textures (especially with chopsticks!).

As this is not a quick fix dieting book and instead intends to promote a healthy and sustainable diet, my recipes do include a healthy amount of rice and noodles. Rice is the natural grain known to contain the least toxins of all, and unlike bread or pasta it does not contain gluten, a gut irritant, and is better to eat than fried carbohydrates or those containing sugar.

Most Asian diets contain starchy carbohydrates, and eating a healthy amount of rice and noodles at mealtimes allows the body to absorb all of the rich vitamins and minerals found in the fish, meat, seaweed, soy and vegetables that you'll also be cooking, and maintain blood sugar levels, therefore limiting snacking. As such, after cooking one of my recipes you will find yourself nourished, satisfied and can rest assured that you will not find yourself reaching for the biscuit tin any time soon!

In general, the Japanese diet conforms to the ideals of 'clean eating' with natural products replacing the artificial wherever possible: miso and soy sauce replacing white salt; rice replacing bread, pasta or other carbohydrate products; fish and tofu replacing fatty red meats; and light, rice or bean-paste based sweets replacing sugary desserts. Still, salt remains one of the areas in which the Japanese diet is less reliable. Although we replace refined salt with seaweed, miso and soya – which have added mineral benefits – all are very high in sodium. I suggest using Japanese tamari rather than soy sauce, which is fermented so it's high in flavour while lower in salt, and always remember it is a seasoning not a sauce.

Finally, I would like to reiterate that this book does not aim to promote fast weight loss, and this is why I have not included calorie counts or nutritional information. One may lose a lot of weight very quickly by avoiding carbohydrates, but it is reversible and unhealthy. The Japanese attitude to eating focuses upon balance and enjoying the powerful flavours of the traditional Japanese palate and this is what I like to encourage: enjoyment of food and enjoyment of a healthy, active and long life. My recipes begin with fresh, nutritious ingredients, remain authentic and draw on generations of experience.

LIVE LONGER

Japan has one of the highest life expectancies in the world; on average, Japanese women live to be 86.61 years old and Japanese men live to be 80.21 years old. There are two reasons for this – one is the advanced medical treatment we receive and the other is undoubtedly the diet. Typically, Japanese meals consist of many small dishes with a variety of different textures and ingredients, eaten very slowly. Most Japanese people tend to eat less meat and dairy products compared to a western diet and take their protein mostly from fish, soya beans and seeds.

Japanese people consume more fish than any other nation and catch the most variety of fish in the world. As a result, oily fish is eaten daily by most Japanese people which in turn means that very few elderly Japanese people suffer from joint problems and allows for an active lifestyle into old age. In fact, in 2015 Misao Okawa, the world's oldest woman, celebrated her 117th birthday in Osaka, western Japan, with her favourite dish of mackerel sushi.

Okawa's favourite dish is not only likely to have led to more mobility into old age, but regular consumption of fish also reduces the likelihood of heart disease and helps preserve grey-matter neurons in the brain, reducing the risk of Alzheimer's disease, cognitive decline and dementia. Furthermore, saltwater fish is the only sun-less source of vitamin D, which scientists say can help ward off disease, promote bone density and mental health.

Another ingredient that sets the Japanese food apart from other cuisines is seaweed, and I often say that my own consumption of seaweed, filled with calcium, is the reason that my hair and nails are so strong and shiny. Containing vitamin A and C, seaweed is also known to be one of the reasons that the Japanese do not wrinkle very early, and it is now included in many modern spa treatments and facial moisturisers.

Not only does seaweed ensure that one looks healthy into old age but the internal benefits are renowned. Sea vegetables, such as seaweed, are known to prevent high blood pressure; have detoxifying benefits, also reducing swelling and promoting digestion; and block chemical oestrogens, therefore working as natural HRT and also helping to prevent breast cancer. Meanwhile, seaweed's most unique benefit is that it is an extraordinary source of a nutrient missing in almost every other food: iodine. Iodine is needed for a healthy thyroid, with a malfunctioning thyroid resulting in a low metabolism, fatigue, muscle weakness, high cholesterol, heart palpitations and impaired memory.

The longevity-promoting effects of a diet including sea vegetables and fish have been heavily researched, mainly through a 25-year study of the Okinawans, the longest-living population in the world. At the southern-most tip of Japan, the Okinawans eat more sea vegetables and soya products than anyone else in the world. As a whole, the Okinawans have a life expectancy of 110 years, and the word 'retirement' does not exist in the traditional Okinawan dialect.

While Okinawa is a rural area, far from my home city of Kyoto or the hustle and bustle of Tokyo, their way of life is wholly Japanese: they prepare meals and eat mindfully; conform to the Japanese saying of '*hara hachi bu*' or 'eat until you are 80 per cent full'; value sleep and relaxation; and exercise into old age.

It is said that the ageing population of Japan is another reason that we focus so closely on the quality of what we eat, as if you live to be 110 years old you will have eaten around 100,000 meals in your lifetime, so it is important that you eat not only to maintain strength, a sharp mind and good health but enjoy the food you eat as well!

THE JAPANESE LANDSCAPE

Japan consists of four main islands across 3,000 kilometres, stretching from Russia to South Korea, with the Sea of Japan and the East China Sea to the west and south-west respectively and the Pacific Ocean to the east: the northernmost island of Hokkaido, the mainland of Honshu, then Shikoku and finally the southern island of Kyushu. These islands are formed from vast ranges of inhabitable mountains – fertile land for growing vegetables, rice, mushrooms, fruits and nuts – that shape the movements of the surrounding seas. This, along with the wide variation of temperatures throughout the archipelago, means that Japanese waters have rather unique currents, leading to one of the largest varieties of fish and crustaceans in the world.

As our climate varies from island to island and province to province, each region has its unique way of preparing what are seen as Japanese signature dishes. For example, if you were to order *okonomiyaki* in Hiroshima you would be presented with a very different dish than if you ordered it in my home city of Kyoto, where the Kansai style is popular. Both are essentially a savoury pancake cooked on a hotplate with a base of egg, flour, cabbage and spring onion, to which you can add any seafood, thinly sliced vegetables or meat (*okonomiyaki* literally meaning 'what you like, grilled'), however if ordering in Kyoto the ingredients are mixed together more like an omelette whereas in Hiroshima all ingredients are layered, with a heavier addition of noodles.

Kyoto is really best known for its tofu, vegetarian Buddhist cuisine and *Kaiseki*, a traditional meal consisting of up to 14 small courses, originating from the dishes served as part of the Japanese tea ceremony in the 16th century, when powdered green tea was found too high in caffeine to consume alone. *Kaiseki* meals have a prescribed order to their dishes. They begin with subtle textures and flavours such as raw sashimi. They might then move on to a vegetable tempura, then a more substantial piece of grilled fish or meat. They then come to a close with rice, a light soup and pickles, before a fresh dessert like a a light sweetened egg custard, *kanten* jelly or often simply fresh fruits. Each dish is savoured and very distinct from the next.

Having been served to the aristocracy in their earliest form, *Kaiseki* meals focus on immaculate presentation, and perhaps it's because I grew up in this region that I have such a passion for the aesthetics of Japanese food. One thing I am sure of is that my love of tofu derives from my childhood in Kyoto, where the soft mountain water allows tofu producers to achieve a silky texture that is chemically impossible to make with hard water, as the water's calcium reacts with the soybean proteins. As you can see, the connection between food and the natural environment in Japan is extremely close, as is the connection of our ingredients to the seasons.

One thing that is consistent to all of Japan's islands is that they experience four distinct seasons. The ingredients we have available, then, not only vary from place to place, but also through the seasons. We call the moment at which a seasonal ingredient is at its best, *shun*. *Shun* to me is the thought of a Japanese strawberry, *ichigo*, at its ripest, glowing red and, in some varieties, the size of an English pear. Or *sanma*, the horse mackerel, which in autumn is absolutely amazing, having just the right amount of fat and juicy flesh; all you need is to grill and eat with grated daikon radish with soy sauce. The use of seasonal produce or *shun* ingredients is one of the most enjoyable ways to cook, and makes one look forward to each new season for what it brings; the 'first spring wind', for example, during which bamboo shoots begin to push through the topsoil, soon to be harvested.

THE JAPANESE FIVE

While we encourage children to eat 30 different ingredients a day, the number five is important in Japanese culture and can be instrumental when forming a healthy attitude to food. The idea of the five principles derives from Zen Buddhist teaching, and while they are often visible on the walls of restaurants that serve temple cuisine, most Japanese people will not be able to recite them.

However, the theme of gratitude and respect instilled by these five principles, or *go-kanmon*, continues to run through Japanese food culture today:

- Be thankful to the force of nature and all human endeavours that have produced this food
- Reflect upon one's own imperfections and do good deeds worthy of deserving food
- Take your position at the table in peace
- Eat for both physical and spiritual nourishment
- Be earnest in the daily struggle for enlightenment

Importantly, when approaching Japanese cuisine, we also use five colours, five ways of preparing and five tastes.

Five Colours

The use of the five colours – white, red, green, yellow and black (or deep purple and brown, the colour of mountain fungi) – boosts nutritional value as each colour offers a different mineral composition. It also ensures a certain mindfulness when preparing a dish. What's more, if you 'eat with your eyes', this attention to presentation means that you will feel more satisfied with less food. It is far easier to continue eating more of a monochrome meal when experiencing just one flavour and texture.

Five Cooking Methods

The five ways of preparing a dish in Japanese cooking are to simmer, grill, steam, fry or pickle. All five are often used for a *Kaiseki* meal, although in home cooking we might make use of four of the five ways

more often than not, perhaps with a hot clear soup, grilled fish, steamed vegetables and rice, and always accompanied by Japanese pickles.

Whether the Japanese home cook achieves every one of the five is less important than balancing flavours. For example, balancing an oily meat dish with a clear soup, or a rich miso-marinated fish dish with a refreshing salad.

Five Tastes

Salty, sweet, sour, bitter and, of course, the renowned Japanese flavour of umami. Umami is a rich and extremely savoury flavour, recently discovered as the tongue's fifth taste. The name comes from the Japanese word *umai*, generally meaning good, well or delicious.

Umami was coined in 1908 as a 'new seasoning' by Japanese chemist Kikunae Ikeda, who had noticed the flavour in various meats and cheeses, but the strongest in dashi stock, which – as you'll soon find in the recipe – is made from kombu seaweed. Kikunae identified umami as the taste of amino acid glutamate, hence the creation of monosodium glutamate (MSG) in the 1980s as an attempt to cheaply recreate umami. Although MSG is an unhealthy and highly addictive product, the fact that the natural umami flavour is so compelling can be positive for health as you can replace salt and sugar with umami for added enjoyment.

True umami flavours are released by slow-cooking, are central to soups, stocks and pickling, and can be found in all sorts of natural ingredients such as dried shiitake mushrooms, soybeans, meat bones, Parmesan cheese, green tea, shrimp and of course seaweed (see page 11 for more on the unique health benefits of sea vegetables).

JAPANESE DINING ETIQUETTE

The name of my company, Hashi, is a play on my maiden name 'Hashimoto' and 'hashi', the Japanese translation of chopsticks. There are a few things that one should remember when using our best-known traditional utensil. Firstly, the Japanese usually place chopsticks horizontally on the chopstick rest. Secondly, if you are eating from a buffet-style meal and a serving spoon or separate chopsticks are not provided, use the reverse end of your chopsticks to pick up the food from the shared plate. You should never serve anyone else with chopsticks. Rather, offer them the bowl or plate to serve themselves.

Also bear in mind that you should never leave a grain of rice on your plate as this is considered impolite in Japan. The Japanese staple diet is rice, and it is polite to show respect to the farmers who provide this food. For the first helping, try to serve yourself a small amount. Then return for more helpings if needed.

When eating sushi or sashimi, avoid mixing the wasabi paste together with the soy sauce. This is thought to kill the flavour of the ingredients. Instead, use a small amount of soy sauce and wasabi with each mouthful; remember that soy sauce is a seasoning agent not a sauce, and the freshness of wasabi – especially freshly grated – is appreciated better when not mixed into soy sauce.

When dipping sushi, also avoid filling up the soy sauce plate to the top (instead aim for around 60 to 70 per cent full), or dipping a whole piece of sushi into itm as this will saturate the whole piece and break up the rice. If it is *nigiri* (hand-moulded) sushi, traditionally you would use clean hands to dip the side with the fish (not the rice side) into the sauce and then taste the fish first not the rice. If you dip the rice side it absorbs too much soy sauce. If it is a *maki* roll, again, use soy sauce sparingly and only dip a corner of the roll into it.

Finally, if someone is pouring you a drink, it is a courtesy to hold your cup or glass up to them. If you are a woman, it is polite to hold your cup or glass with both hands, and when pouring a drink to hold the bottle in the same way.

ABOUT THE BOOK

The aim of this book is to provide an array of dishes that promote a sustainable, slimming diet and long, healthy lifestyle, and encourage the use of Japanese food as a tool for healthy living. It looks primarily at the health benefits of the Japanese diet – namely a slimmer physique, stable blood sugar, increased joint flexibility and a long lifespan – and which ingredients contribute to each.

This book is for everyone, offering reassurance and easy-to-follow steps for the beginner and healthy alternatives to the repertoire of a seasoned Japanese cook. As you will see in the equipment and ingredients sections (pages 14 and 18), and contrary to popular belief, to cook Japanese cuisine you do not need an entirely new kitchen or indeed many different gadgets. Japanese cooking uses the same set of ingredients repeatedly, and most of these ingredients can be easily found in your local supermarket.

Within the basics section (page 28), I've given master recipes for stocks and staples, and how to prepare unfamiliar ingredients. I believe that using these often helps to master the core flavours of Japanese cooking. The sections in the book are divided by the main ingredient of the dishes. You'll find that some vegetable dishes may contain tofu and some rice dishes may contain fish, but it should be intuitive which is the main ingredient in each case.

EQUIPMENT AND UTENSILS

Bamboo Sushi Mat (*Makisu*)
This is essential equipment when making sushi rolls.
It is made from strips of bamboo and extremely
durable. Wash with hot water.

Chopping Board (*Manaita*)
There are several types of chopping boards available.
For hygiene purposes, glass or plastic are common
for domestic use. However, professional Japanese
chefs prefer to use wooden chopping boards as
these are thought to be gentler on the knives and the
ingredients don't tend to slip like on other materials,
i.e. when cutting fish.

Clay Pot (*Donabe*)
A clay pot specially used for *nabe* hotpot dishes. A
Japanese version of fondue, *nabe* is cooked at the
table where diners add their own fresh ingredients
to the simmering broth. *Nabe* clay pots are available
in many different sizes ranging from a small one
portion pot to a larger one that serves 10–12 people.
A *donabe* is often used for winter dishes as it keeps
the food hot. It is also ovenproof.

Cooking Chopsticks (*Ryori Bashi*)
Made from strong bamboo, and extremely durable
to high heat, cooking chopsticks are longer than
your ordinary ones. Perfect for using when deep-
frying foods.

Fan (*Uchiwa*)
A Japanese fan is useful not only for cooling off
oneself, but also to quickly cool down rice when
mixing in the vinegar for sushi rice.

Ginger Grater and Daikon Grater (*Oroshiki*)
Using a very fine-toothed Japanese grater for grating
ginger produces an extremely fine and creamy
texture. The coarser side of the grater is used to grate
daikon radish, a Japanese radish, or *mooli*. Both
grated ginger and daikon radish are often used to
garnish many dishes.

Japanese Omelette Pan (*Tamago-yaki*)
A small, rectangular pan used to make Japanese
omelettes for domestic use. A larger square one is
used in industrial kitchens. Japanese egg rolls or
Tamago-yaki (page 179) cannot be made as well
without this pan.

Knives (*Houcho*)
Many types of knives are used in the Japanese
kitchen. The all-purpose knife is most commonly
used in the domestic kitchen whereas in the
professional kitchen on average 10–15 different types
are used. It is important to sharpen the knife with a
stone sharpener.

Mortar and Pestle (*Suribachi*)
Unlike Western mortar and pestles, the Japanese
suribachi has a rough grating surface inside the bowl.
The pestle is made from a hard wood, perfect for
achieving very fine grinds.

Noodle/Rice Bowls (*Donburi*)
These are a staple in the Japanese household as soups, noodles and rice with toppings are a regular meal. Usually noodle/rice bowls will measure about 20cm wide and 12cm deep.

Rice Cooker (*Suihanki*)
Although you can cook rice in a heavy-based pan, if you eat rice at least once or twice a week it is worth investing in a rice cooker as this will make your life a hundred times easier. In the Japanese kitchen, a rice cooker is considered an essential item.

Sashimi Knife (*Sashimi Boucho*)
As the name suggests, this knife is used to slice raw fish. Sharpened only on one side and usually about 24cm long, the blade gives a long clean cut in one stroke.

Sharpening Stone (*Toishi*)
This is a rectangular natural stone used to sharpen Japanese knives. It is important to maintain and sharpen knives regularly, especially if you have invested in a good-quality one.

Sushi Barrel (*Handai* or *Hangiri*)
This round, flat-bottomed wooden barrel is the key to making authentic sushi rice. Using the *handai* sushi barrel or rice bowl, *shamoji* wooden spatula and *uchiwa* fan in combination during the final steps makes a real difference and is a must if you want to achieve the ultimate sushi rice.

Tempura Pan (*Tempura Nabe*)
For use with dishes that are deep-fried. It comes with a rack that you can rest just-cooked ingredients on attached to the top of the pan so that the oil can drip back into the pan. The tempura pan is the Japanese version of a deep-fat fryer.

Wooden Spatula (*Shamoji*)
A large, flat spoon used for scooping and mixing rice. Bamboo, wood or plastic spatulas all do the trick.

Wooden Sushi Mould (*Oshi Zushi* or *Hako Zushi Kata*)
The rectangular wooden mould is handy for making compressed sushi. Traditionally, this mould is soaked in water before use to prevent sushi rice sticking. However, a new and easy way to prevent the rice from sticking instead of soaking the mould is to put a layer of cling film between the mould and the rice.

Author's Note
You can find a wonderful selection of utensils and crockery online or in specialist shops. I often use Doki Japanese Tableware in London, who stock a huge array of Japanese ceramics in their brilliant shop. To find out more visit dokiltd.co.uk.

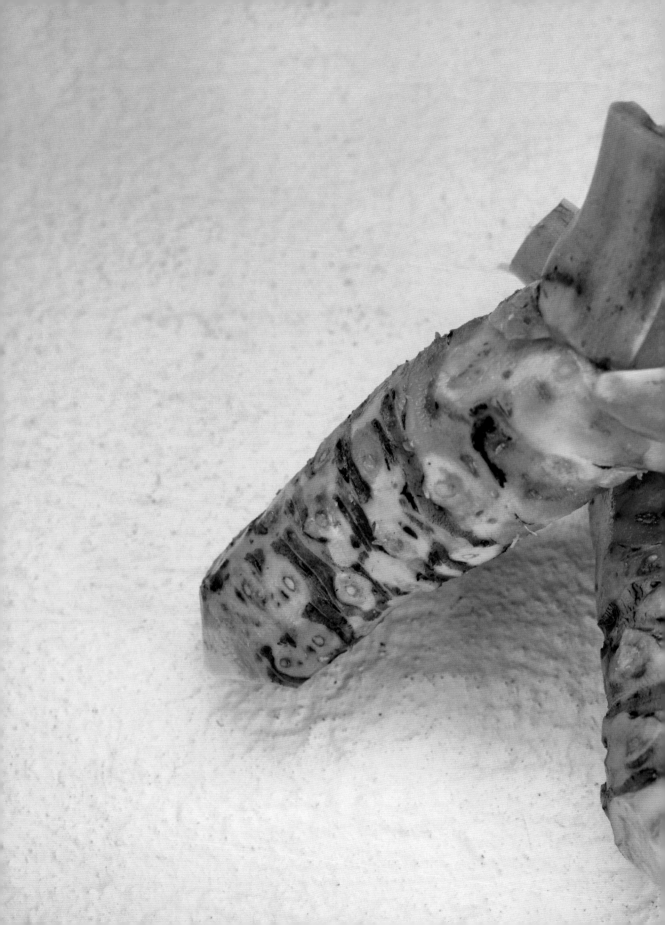

STORECUPBOARD INGREDIENTS

Bonito Flakes (*Katsuobushi*)
These are dried shavings or flakes of a fish called Pacific bonito. Larger, coarser flakes are used to make dashi, whilst finer shavings are used as a garnish.

Brown Rice (*Genmai*)
Genmai rice is the least polished and the most nutritious rice. It is high in fibre, takes much longer to cook and is chewier and nutty compared to white rice.

Chilli-Infused Sesame Oil (*Rahyu*)
This is often used for Chinese and Japanese fusion dishes such as gyoza and ramen.

Dried Seaweed Powder (*Ao-nori*)
This is a condiment for sprinkling. It has a strong flavour of seaweed and is bright green in colour.

Japanese Horseradish (*Wasabi*)
Although this is a type of horseradish, it is somewhat different to the Western variety. The root of Japanese horseradish is much smaller and pale green in colour. Ready-made pastes or dried forms of wasabi are widely available, however the actual wasabi content present is often extremely low. Fresh wasabi is available online in the UK now and I source mine from The Wasabi Company, who are the only UK growers of wasabi: www.thewasabicompany.co.uk.

Japanese Mayonnaise (*Mayonaisu*)
Japanese mayonnaise is much more yellow in colour than the typical Western mayonnaise. As the colour shows, Japanese mayonnaise contains more egg yolks. It is also creamier and has a more citrusy flavour.

Noodles (*Men*)
Soba – brown buckwheat noodles. The healthiest of all the noodles. You can also obtain different flavours such as green tea or yuzu.
Somen – fine white wheat flour noodles.
Hiyamugi – medium white wheat flour noodles.
Udon – thick white wheat flour noodles.
Kishimen – flat white wheat flour noodles.

Ramen – originally from China, and made of wheat flour and eggs.

Red Beans (*Adzuki*)
Adzuki beans are grown in Japan and China, and are smaller versions of kidney beans. In Asia they are often used in sweet dishes.

Rice (*Kome*)
Short- or medium-grain rice is most suitable for Japanese dishes. Any kind of rice from Japan should be the right kind. Alternatively, short-grain rice from California, Australia, Spain and Korea are available in the UK and are also suitable.

Rice Vinegar (*Komezu*)
Rice vinegar is milder than most Western vinegars. It is mainly used for sushi rice, salad dressings and some simmered dishes. Cider vinegar can be substituted with a little water added.

Rice Wine (*Sake*)
This is a dry rice wine, used for both cooking and drinking. Traditionally, sake is drunk hot with a cold dish, such as sushi and sashimi, but it can be drunk cold as well.

Sansho Pepper (*Sansho*)
The *sansho* or prickly ash tree also yields fragrant *kinome* leaves, which are often used as a garnish. Earthy, tangy and lemony in flavour, when these leaves are placed directly on your tongue, you'll notice a sort of tingling sensation. Sansho is usually sold ground and typically used on grilled foods such as *yakitori* chicken or eel as it goes well with teriyaki sauce.

Seaweed (*Kaisou*)

Sea kelp (kombu) – this should be thick, hard and black or very dark green. You may notice a white powdery surface – this is salt. There is no need to rinse the kombu, just wipe with kitchen paper. Kombu is one of the two vital ingredients for making dashi stock.

Wakame – the most commonly used seaweed in Japan. It is usually sold in dry form and is often used in soups and salads. You can also buy fresh wakame, which is used in simmering dishes.

Hijiki – the second most popular seaweed. Dried, hijiki forms pointy very thin shards. Before use, soak it in a bowl of water for 30 minutes. Unlike wakame, hijiki is ideal when simmered slowly in a dish, allowing the flavours to deepen and develop.

Arame – a long noodle-like seaweed. The flavour is similar to kombu but softer and easier to cook. Similar to hijiki, arame is best simmered.

Dulse – a beautiful purple-hued seaweed that is often treated as a salad. It is best eaten raw, after soaking in water for 10–15 minutes.

Sesame Seeds (*Goma*)

There are two types of sesame seeds used in Japanese cooking – white and black. White ones are untoasted and black ones are toasted. If you are using white sesame seeds in a dish, simply toast the seeds in a small dry pan until they become golden in colour. Toasting enhances the flavour of the seeds.

Seven-Spice Powder (*Shichimi*)

This is widely used at the Japanese table as a dried condiment. The mixture of seven spices also includes chilli as a dominant ingredient. Most often used as a condiment for noodle soups, grilled fish and meat.

Soy Bean Paste (*Miso*)

There are many types of *miso*, a fermented soy bean paste. *Miso* is mostly used for soups but also for marinades, sauces and salad dressings. Generally, the darker in colour the miso paste is, the saltier. Varieties include the toffee-coloured koji *miso*, along with red *miso* and white *miso*. *Miso* paste can be kept in an airtight container in the refrigerator for up to about 1 year but tends to get saltier as it ages.

Soy Sauce (*Sho-yu*)

Soy sauce or *sho-yu* is a basic ingredient used in most Japanese dishes and it is the salt agent. *Sho-yu* means Japanese soy sauce and it is much less salty than the Chinese soy sauce. *Tamari* is another type of Japanese soy sauce and it is gluten free.

Sticky Rice Cakes (*Mochi*)

Traditionally, *mochi* is made with special sticky rice called *mochigome*, which is steamed and then pounded and kneaded repeatedly. You can obtain ready-cooked and vacuum-packed ones in Japanese supermarkets.

Stock (*Dashi*)

Traditionally, three types of dashi stock are used in Japanese cooking. The most commonly used dashi is made with two ingredients, namely bonito flakes (*katsuobushi*) and sea kelp (*kombu*). This type of dashi is used in many Japanese dishes. The other two types of dashi are not as commonly used and are either made with little fish similar to anchovies (*niboshi*) or with dried shiitake mushrooms.

Stock Powder (*Dashi no moto*)

Instant dashi stock is available in powder form or liquid concentrate. It is used daily by Japanese people. Simply stir the powder or liquid into boiling water.

Sushi Vinegar (*Sushizu*)

This is a special blend of rice vinegar, sugar, salt and dashi. A bottle of ready-to-use sushi vinegar is available in liquid form or in a sachet in powdered form.

Sweetened rice wine (*Mirin*)

This is a sweet rice wine used for cooking only.

Toasted Seaweed (*Yakinori*)

This is used for rolling sushi or to wrap around rice balls (*onigiri*). It is available as small paper-like sheets or shredded for using to sprinkle. Keep it in an airtight container in a cool, dry place.

FRESH INGREDIENTS

VEGETABLES

Bamboo Shoot (*Takenoko*)
These are one of the classic ingredients of East Asia. The uniqueness of the crisp texture makes this mountain vegetable special, although it contains very few nutrients. This crisp texture will increase dramatically if the bamboo is fresh and in season.

Chinese Cabbage (*Hakusai*)
As the name suggests, this cabbage was originally introduced into Japan from China. In recent years, this has become one of the most popular leafy vegetables in Japanese cooking, as it is very versatile. Chinese cabbage is often used for pot dishes or lightly pickled and served as a condiment.

Chrysanthemum Leaves (*Shungiku*)
Originally grown in the Mediterranean coastal area, in recent years they have become popular in Asia. Chrysanthemum leaves are often used in *nabe* dishes in Japan and as the stem part is quite hard to bite through leaves can be eaten as salad.

Daikon radish
Daikon (or *mooli*) is a long white radish. It is one of the most versatile vegetables and can be used for soups, salads and pickles. It is widely used as a sashimi garnish (shredded) or a tempura condiment (grated).

Ginger (*Shoga*)
Shoga or fresh root ginger is the most commonly used spice in Japan and it is also used in many other cuisines worldwide. *Shoga* is considered to be a healthy product as well as being a great flavouring for many dishes. As ginger is known to help digestion, it's often used with oily fish and meat to help break down the fat. *Shoga* can be served freshly grated or thinly sliced, and raw or cooked, in many dishes. The most popular way to eat ginger in the West is as pickled ginger accompanied by sushi.

Japanese Pumpkin (*Kabocha*)
A deep green, ragged-skinned pumpkin that is much smaller than the Western pumpkin. The flesh is very dense and deep orange in colour and is a good source of nutrients. This is traditionally used in side dishes (simmered in broth) and for tempura. In more recent years, Japanese pumpkin is often used for soups and desserts (combined with other non-Japanese ingredients such as butter and cream, making the desserts very calorific).

Lotus Root (*Renkon*)
The lotus root usually has three or four sections and looks a little like a large uneven sausage. When cut, it has several, large vertical holes. Although not distinctive in terms of flavour, it is enjoyed for its crunch and texture.

Shiso
This is the most popular herb for Japanese cooking. The shape of the leaf is similar to nettle and the flavour is very distinctive. Shiso is a Japanese version of coriander or basil. It is often used as a garnish for sashimi and other fresh dishes. Shiso-flavoured ready-made salad dressing is also available to buy from Japanese supermarkets.

Spinach (*Horensou*)
Japanese spinach is much firmer than the typical variety found in the UK, with reddish-coloured stems closer to the roots. It is normally displayed in a bunch with the roots attached in the shops and supermarkets. The stems are highly nutritious and packed with flavour.

Spring Onions (*Negi*)
There are two types of spring onions in Japan. One is very long and thick, like the Western leek. The other one is thinner, but not as small and fine as spring onions in the West. This is used for many dishes either as a garnish or just to add flavour.

Sweet Potato (*Satsumaimo*)
This is a long-shaped sweet potato with a light, burgundy-coloured skin. The flesh is pale yellow and the texture is somewhere between pumpkin and potato. It is more glutinous than potato. 'Satsuma' is the old name for the southern region of Japan. 'Imo' means potato.

Yuzu

Yuzu (or Japanese lime/mandarin) is regarded as a precious citrus fruit for Japanese cooking. Being a seasonal citrus fruit, its rarity makes yuzu even more popular. It is used not only in cooking but as a fragrance for bath products in Japan, being believed to be good for the skin. Fresh yuzu is difficult to get hold of outside of Japan, but concentrated yuzu juice is available in bottles.

MUSHROOMS AND SOYBEAN PRODUCTS

Deep-Fried Tofu Sheets (*Aburaage*)

This is a golden-coloured, deep-fried bean curd. Japanese deep-fried tofu comes as rectangular, flat sheets, each sheet weighing about 20g. There are many different uses for this versatile product, such as for soups, simmered dishes, sushi, etc. As the inside is hollow and the *aburaage* has a durable texture, this makes it ideal for stuffing with things such as minced meat, egg, rice and so on.

Dried Soybean Skin (*Yuba*)

Yuba is the dried soybean skin that forms on the surface of soybean milk during the tofu making process. In Japan, you can find fresh *yuba*, which, with its beautiful creamy texture and rich sweet tofu flavour, is a delicacy in its own right. It is also extremely light. My hometown, Kyoto, is well-known for tofu, especially *yuba*.

Enoki

These are interesting shaped mushrooms that have become very popular in the West in recent years. Enoki have tiny ivory-coloured caps with very thin stalks and a crunchy texture. They are used more for their texture rather than their very subtle flavour.

Eringi

It's called king mushroom in UK as it's king size. Unlike other mushrooms, it is solid and hard. Eringi are best sliced, then fried or grilled. It's meaty and has a nice crunchy bite.

Fermented Soybeans (*Natto*)

These fermented soybeans are rather smelly and slimy and not the most favoured food to the Western palette. *Natto* has been a constant in the Japanese diet, and is traditionally known as the most nutritious breakfast food. *Natto* is usually eaten with freshly cooked plain rice, raw egg yolk, dashi *sho-yu* and spring onions.

Shiitake

The most well-known type of Japanese mushroom. Dark brown, with a velvety cap of about 5cm in diameter and short stalks. Shiitake mushrooms are available in both fresh and dried forms and both are widely used in Japanese cooking.

Shimeji

This is another popular Japanese mushroom. It grows in bunches and has small, light brownish-grey caps and fat stalks. The flavour is quite subtle but their unique appearance and the firm texture makes them a popular choice.

Tofu

Tofu is fresh bean curd and it is one of the staple foods in the Japanese diet as it is highly nutritious and low in fat. Tofu is an ivory-coloured soybean product with a firm custard texture, available either as fresh or vacuum-packed. Silken tofu or *kinu* has a more delicate and soft texture than cotton tofu or *momen*, which has a firm, rough texture. Silken tofu tends to be used for soup and eaten as fresh, whereas the cotton tofu is used for simmered recipes and for frying. In recipes, we refer to silken tofu or firm tofu (which is the cotton tofu).

Young Soybeans (*Edamame*)

Young soybeans in their hairy pods. You can obtain half cooked and frozen ones in the supermarket throughout the year. In Japan, fresh ones appear in the market at the beginning of the summer with the stalks attached. These are becoming increasingly popular outside of Japan as a simple nibble with drinks. Traditionally they are just boiled with salted water and served with a sprinkling of salt.

DRINKS

TEAS

Bancha

Bancha is made up of large leaves and stems. The dried leaves are almost brown in colour and it is drunk daily cold and/or hot and served with meals.

Genmaicha

A mixture of bancha and roasted rice grains. The nutty toasted rice grains add an extremely pleasing aroma.

Gyokuro

Gyokuro is the best leaf tea made from young leaves freshly picked in early spring, and one of the most expensive. The dried leaves are shiny and deep green in colour. Gyokuro should be brewed in warm water, about 50–60°C in small quantities. It is extraordinarily fragrant, sweet and mellow at the same time.

Hojicha

Hojicha is a roasted bancha and has a slightly nuttier and smokier flavour profile. The dried leaves are brownish in colour.

Matcha

A powdered tea traditionally used for formal tea ceremonies. Dried and flattened tea leaves are ground to a powder that retains the vivid green and fragrant properties of green tea. In recent years, matcha has made a comeback being used for many sweet dishes. It is also one of the most popular ice cream flavours in Japan.

Mugicha

'Mugi' means barley and this is actually roasted barley. Strictly speaking it's not a tea. Many Japanese households keep mugicha in the fridge during the summer months and drink it like water as it is healthy and caffeine free.

Sencha

Sencha is a mid-range leaf tea made from young and good-quality leaves. Most Japanese households keep sencha for serving guests with Japanese sweets.

ALCOHOLIC DRINKS

Beer

In Japan, beer is the most common drink of choice to accompany a meal. Asahi, Sapporo and Kirin are the three major beer companies and they export worldwide. Japanese beer tends to be light and refreshing.

Sake

Sake is made from a harder variety of rice and can be drunk cold or warm depending on your preference. The alcohol content is around 15 per cent – very mild and easy to drink with a meal. Sake is also one of the basic ingredients used in Japanese cooking.

Shochu

Shochu is distilled spirit made from rice, grains or potatoes. Originally, it was considered a cheap alternative to sake but recently it has become quite fashionable among young people and often used for making cocktails for its high alcohol content.

Umeshu

Ume is a Japanese plum. To make the wine, unripened apricots are soaked in a mixture of clear alcoholic spirit (such as sake or shochu) and sugar for at least 3 months. Because of its intense sweetness, it is often drunk as an aperitif.

Whisky

The Japanese whisky industry started up nearly 100 years ago by Suntory at Yamazaki in Kyoto. Whisky has consistently been a popular drink among Japanese for many decades. It is often drunk after dinner with water and ice, which is called *mizuwari*.

BASICS AND SAUCES

DASHI STOCK
(USING SEA KELP AND BONITO FLAKES)

MAKES ABOUT 1.1 LITRES

20g dried sea kelp (kombu or konbu)
1.2 litres cold water, plus 55ml cold
   water
20g bonito flakes

Place the sea kelp in a bowl, pour over 1.2 litres cold water and leave to soak for between 2–5 hours. Transfer the soaked sea kelp and soaking water to a pan and bring to the boil. Just before the mixture begins to boil, remove the sea kelp using a slotted spoon and discard. Boil the liquid for 1 minute.

Add the bonito flakes to the pan and bring back to the boil, removing the pan from the heat just before the mixture comes to the boil. Stir in the additional 55ml cold water to cool the mixture down a little.

Allow the bonito flakes to settle on the bottom of pan, then strain the dashi stock through a muslin-lined (or kitchen paper-lined) sieve or fine mesh colander (you must not squeeze the muslin or paper to get out as much liquid as possible – just let it drip!).

Use the dashi stock as required. Store the cooled dashi stock in an airtight container in the fridge for up to 3 days or in the freezer for up to 3 months.

VEGETARIAN STOCK

MAKES ABOUT 1.1 LITRES

15g dried sea kelp (kombu or konbu)
15g dried shiitake mushrooms
1.2 litres cold water

Place the sea kelp and shiitake mushrooms in separate bowls. Add 600ml cold water to each bowl and leave to soak for between 2–5 hours.

Transfer the soaked sea kelp and soaking water to a pan and bring to the boil. Just before the mixture begins to boil, remove the sea kelp using a slotted spoon and discard. Boil the liquid for 1 minute, then remove from the heat and pour the liquid into a suitable container. Set aside.

Repeat the same procedure with the soaked mushrooms and their soaking liquid in the same pan.

Combine the sea kelp liquid and the mushroom liquid in a pan, bring to the boil and boil for 1 minute. Remove from the heat and allow the mixture to cool slightly. If the liquid contains small bits from the mushrooms, strain the stock through a muslin-lined (or kitchen paper-lined) sieve or fine mesh colander. Discard any bits from the sieve.

Use the stock as required. Store the cooled stock in an airtight container in the fridge for up to 3 days or in the freezer for up to 3 months.

NOODLE BROTH

MAKES ABOUT 950ML

1 litre dashi stock (page 28)
4 tablespoons mirin
6 tablespoons soy sauce
2 tablespoons sake
1 tablespoon sugar
¼ teaspoon sea salt

Combine all the ingredients in a saucepan and bring to
just below boiling. Heat gently for 5–6 minutes, uncovered,
until the sugar has dissolved. Use hot, warm or cold,
as required.

PLAIN RICE

MAKES ABOUT 950G COOKED
RICE

480g short-grain white rice
about 715ml cold water

Place the rice in a sieve and wash it thoroughly using cold
water until the water runs almost clear, allowing the rice
to drain before rinsing again. When you first rinse the
rice, the water looks like coconut milk which is the starch
coming out of the rice. You need to get rid of as much
starch as possible. Repeat the rinsing and draining process
at least 3–4 times until the water becomes almost clear.

Place the drained rice and measured cold water (you need
roughly 10 per cent more water than the volume/quantity
of rice) in a heavy-based saucepan (choose the size of the
pan assuming that the rice will increase by about three
times its original volume). Leave the rice to soak in the
cold water for at least 30 minutes.

Place the pan containing the soaked rice over a high heat.
Cover the pan with a lid (ideally the lid has a tiny hole on
the top or the side to release a little steam; if not, wrap the
lid with a towel, which will absorb most of the steam) and
bring the water to the boil. Once boiling, reduce the heat
to the lowest setting and simmer for about 13–17 minutes
or until all the water is absorbed (the timing for this
depends on several things, for example, the quantity of rice
you are cooking, what kind of pan you are using, which
type of short-grain rice you are using and so on). You must
keep the lid closed at all times as the steaming process is
very important. If you keep opening the lid to check, you
are releasing an important amount of steam every time –
so you need to be very patient!

Remove the pan from the heat and allow the rice to stand
and steam for a further 15 minutes with the lid tightly
closed. If you are using an electric hob, you must move the
pan off the hob, otherwise the rice will cook further.

SUSHI RICE

Cooked sushi rice is always served at room temperature (unless specified otherwise in a recipe).

**MAKES ABOUT 600–700G
COOKED SUSHI RICE**

For the sushi rice
320g short-grain white rice
550ml cold water

For the sushi vinegar
110ml rice vinegar
60g caster sugar
½ teaspoon salt
½ teaspoon concentrated dashi stock
   (page 28) or instant dashi powder

Necessary utensils
a large, flat wooden bowl/barrel
a large, flat wooden spatula
a fan

To prepare and cook the sushi rice, follow the instructions given on page 29 for cooking plain rice.

Meanwhile, put all the ingredients for the sushi vinegar in a saucepan and heat gently, stirring occasionally. Remove the pan from the heat and set aside to cool.

Wet the inside of the wooden bowl and the wooden spatula with cold water (this will help to prevent the rice from sticking to the utensils).

Transfer the steaming hot cooked rice to the wooden bowl and spread it evenly in the bowl.

Gradually pour in the sushi vinegar, folding the mixture with the wooden spatula as if you are cutting through the lumps of rice and separating the grains at a sharp angle. You must fold not stir the rice, otherwise the rice grains will become crushed and lumpy. Continue folding the rice gently, while fanning the rice using your other hand (another person's help here is very handy!) until the rice is at room temperature. Fanning is very important as it is the most efficient way to cool the temperature of the rice quickly. Once ready, the rice should be shiny and sticky but still with separate grains. Cover the rice with a piece of damp muslin cloth until you are ready to use it. This will stop the rice from drying out and becoming hardened.

TERIYAKI SAUCE

MAKES ABOUT 500ML

375ml soy sauce
250ml mirin
90g sugar

Combine all the ingredients in a saucepan and bring to the boil. Reduce the heat and simmer, uncovered, for 20–30 minutes, or until thickened and the consistency of double cream. Use hot, warm or cold, as required.

JAPANESE MAYONNAISE

MAKES ABOUT 300ML

2 medium egg yolks
1 teaspoon rice vinegar
1 teaspoon lemon juice
¼ teaspoon sea salt
1 teaspoon sugar
1 teaspoon Dijon mustard
200ml rapeseed oil

Whisk all the ingredients except the oil in a bowl. Begin drizzling in the oil, little by little, whisking all the time, until thickened and mayonnaise-like. This will keep for at least a few days if stored in an airtight jar.

SMALL BITES

One of the key characteristics of the Japanese diet is our love of many dishes and a variety of flavours, and so our cuisine is perfect for canapés and small bites. I began my Canapé Classes several years ago and at first I wasn't sure how popular they would be, although it seems that the demand for an alternative to the infamous smoked salmon blini is high and so I'm thrilled that I continue to be able to teach new canapés on a weekly basis.

I pride myself on teaching truly authentic Japanese cuisine, although fusion food is incredibly enjoyable to experiment with and where better to experiment than with small bites? Most of my small dishes are influenced by my travels around the world before I settled in London; for example incorporating Italian textures in my arancini balls, Spanish ingredients with my padron peppers and British favourites with my parsnip mash. In pairing unusual flavours such as sharp watercress with sweet ponzu sauce, this series of recipes illustrates how simple it is to bring Japanese flavours into dishes that might already be part of your cooking repertoire.

These dishes are designed to look and taste beautiful, to be simple to prepare on the day or in advance, and significantly they are easy to eat too! This means that you can either serve them at home alongside a small Japanese vegetable dish or salad, or pair with wine or sake during a lively dinner party – in any case, your guests are sure to be impressed by being offered something a little different.

You might be surprised to find some of these recipes in a book that is designed to encourage healthy living, however the Japanese are not afraid of carbohydrates in moderation, and that is exactly what small bites allow you to enjoy: heavier ingredients in small amounts, which is a very healthy attitude in my opinion.

VENISON TATAKI WITH WASABI PARSNIP MASH

There is a fantastic harmony of flavours in this dish; the rich venison paired with the sweet parsnip and hot, fresh wasabi. It is a luxurious little plate to start off a meal.

SERVES 4

cooking oil, for brushing

320g venison fillet

4 tablespoons soy sauce

4 tablespoons mirin

1 tablespoon vegetable or sunflower oil

2 onions, very thinly sliced

2 tablespoons deep-fried shallots (page 79 or shop-bought)

handful of watercress

For the wasabi parsnip mash

1 tablespoon vegetable or sunflower oil

2 medium parsnips, peeled and cut into 2cm cubes

75ml soy milk

20g lightly salted butter

1–2 teaspoons freshly grated wasabi or prepared wasabi paste

Heat 1 tablespoon oil in a frying pan over low heat. Add the parsnip to the pan, cover with a sheet of foil and fry gently for 8–10 minutes. Turn the pieces over and cook, covered, for a further 6–7 minutes, or until the parsnip is tender.

Transfer the parsnip to a blender or food processor with the soy milk and butter, and blitz until smooth. Add the wasabi gradually until you reach your preferred level of hotness.

Heat a frying pan over high heat. Brush the venison fillet with a little oil and sear all surfaces of the meat. Turn the heat down to medium and cook one side for about 3 minutes and then turn over and cook the other side for another 3 minutes (to achieve medium-rare). In a bowl, mix the soy sauce and mirin. Take the venison out of the pan and then transfer to the bowl of soy sauce and mirin, basting well and making sure both sides of the meat are coated. Leave to rest and come to room temperature.

Heat the vegetable or sunflower oil in the pan used to cook the venison over medium heat and fry the onions for 7–8 minutes, or until they are softened and translucent. Pour the soy sauce and mirin mixture (which the beef has been soaked in) into the pan and cook for 3 minutes, until the onions have absorbed the liquid ingredients but still have a little bite.

Slice the venison very thinly. To assemble the dish, firstly, plate the wasabi parsnip and then arrange the sliced venison and caramelised onions on top. Garnish with deep-fried shallots and a little watercress. This works well served on side plates or canapé spoons.

MISO GINGER PEA PATTIES

Patties are simple and tasty little snacks, which can easily be prepared the night before. Try cooking these up for breakfast instead of reaching for cereal. They are a revelation.

SERVES 4 (MAKES 20)

300g podded fresh peas or frozen
   peas
60g streaky bacon, finely chopped
½ onion, grated
1 tablespoon grated ginger
ground black pepper
2 tablespoons plain flour
2 eggs, lightly beaten
2 teaspoons miso paste
2 tablespoons sunflower oil
coriander or watercress, to garnish,
   optional

Bring a saucepan of water to the boil and cook the peas for 3 minutes. Drain, transfer to a bowl and use a stick blender to purée, leaving a little texture so it's not completely smooth.

Add the bacon, onion and ginger and season with the pepper. Sift in the flour and add the lightly beaten eggs and miso. Mix the ingredients well.

Heat the oil in a large frying pan over medium heat and, using 2 teaspoons, drop portions of the mixture into the pan. Flatten the mixture with the back of a spoon. Repeat until the pan is full of patties (don't overcrowd the pan) and fry, in batches, for about 2 minutes on each side or until cooked through and lightly browned. Use a slotted spoon to remove the patties from the pan and drain on kitchen paper. Serve immediately, garnished with coriander or watercress if you like.

PLUM AND GINGER PORK IN LETTUCE CUPS

This dish is perfect for preparing in advance; just throw it all together at the last minute. Rich and spicy pork goes perfectly with crunchy lettuce.

SERVES 4

4–6 little gem lettuces
4 medium dried shiitake mushrooms, finely chopped
1 tablespoon vegetable, corn or sunflower oil
1 garlic clove, peeled and grated
30g ginger, peeled and grated
45g finely chopped spring onions
250g minced pork
1 teaspoon chilli paste
1 teaspoon cornflour mixed with 1 tablespoon mushroom soaked water
handful of coriander leaves
toasted sesame seeds, for sprinkling

For the sauce
1 teaspoon plum sauce
1 teaspoon oyster sauce
1 tablespoon mirin
1 teaspoon sesame oil

Remove and discard the outer leaves of the little gem lettuces. Separate the leaves and keep the smaller inner leaves for a salad. Wash the leaves under cold running water, drain well in a colander and keep in the fridge.

Soak the mushrooms in warm water for 30 minutes. Adding a teaspoon of sugar to the water will help plump up the mushrooms.

Mix the sauce ingredients in a bowl and set aside.

Heat the oil in a wok or large frying pan, add the garlic, ginger and spring onions, and stir-fry for 30 seconds. Add the minced pork and let it cook until it changes to pale brown in colour.

Drain the mushrooms, reserving 1 tablespoon of the liquid to mix with the cornflour and discard the rest. Add the mushrooms and the chilli paste to the wok or frying pan and cook for 1 minute.

Add the plum sauce mixture and cook over a medium heat for 2–3 minutes, or until most of the liquid has evaporated. Turn up the heat and add the cornflour mixture and cook for 2 minutes, until the pork mixture becomes quite dense. Turn off the heat and allow to cool slightly.

Scoop the pork mixture into the individual lettuce leaves and sprinkle with coriander leaves and toasted sesame seeds. Serve warm or at room temperature.

CRISPY PRAWN WONTONS

There is just something about wontons – they are so hearty and moreish. Don't be alarmed by the number of ingredients; all you need to do is chop, wrap and cook. It really is as easy as that.

MAKES ABOUT 40 PIECES

50 pastry wonton wrappers
750ml vegetable or sunflower oil, for
   shallow-frying

For the filling
100g squid or firm white fish fillet,
   roughly chopped
150g prawns, deshelled, deveined
   and finely chopped
100g tinned bamboo shoots, drained
   and finely chopped
2 tablespoons finely chopped spring
   onions
1 egg white
1–2 teaspoons cornflour
½ teaspoon salt
½ teaspoon sugar
pinch of ground white pepper
1 teaspoon soy sauce
2–4 teaspoons sake
2 teaspoons sesame oil
1 teaspoon grated ginger

For the dipping sauce
2 tablespoons rice vinegar
1 tablespoon fish sauce
1 tablespoon soy sauce
1 teaspoon finely chopped red chilli
3 tablespoons clear honey
3 tablespoons lemon juice

Put the squid (or white fish) in a food processor and blitz until smooth. Tip into a large bowl along with the remaining ingredients for the filling and mix well until completely combined and almost elastic in texture.

Take a wrapper in one hand, scoop out a teaspoon-sized ball of the filling and place in the centre of the wrapper. Dab a little water around the edges of the wrapper, then fold in the edges making pleats as if wrapping an Easter egg with wrapping paper. Pinch and seal the top to secure the filling.

Heat the oil in a wok or large, deep frying pan to around 160°C/320°F. To test whether the oil is the right temperature, drop a corner of a wrapper into the pan – it should bounce back slowly.

Use chopsticks to carefully slide a few dumplings into the hot oil at a time, taking care to dip the filling-filled part (the base of the dumplings) into the oil first, submerging it in the oil for a few seconds until the filling is cooked. Flip over and let the rest of the wonton crisp up. Remove the wontons and drain on kitchen paper. Repeat the process of frying the wontons until all are cooked.

Mix all the ingredients for the dipping sauce in a bowl and then serve together with the wontons.

CALAMARI AND WATERCRESS TEMPURA

This has been one of my top three canapés of all time. It is simple to prepare and a fuss-free way to enjoy tempura seafood and vegetables with family and friends. Here, the citrusy ponzo sauce cuts through the richness of the deep-fried morsels.

SERVES 4

½ leek
50g watercress, tough stalks
    discarded
100g tempura flour
115ml ice-cold water
200g calamari, sliced into 1cm pieces
1 litre sunflower or vegetable oil, for
    deep-frying

For the ponzo dipping sauce
3 tablespoons soy sauce
2 tablespoons rice vinegar
1 tablespoon mirin
1 teaspoon sugar
1 tablespoon lime juice
1 onion, finely grated

At least 1 hour before serving, mix all the ingredients for the dipping sauce. You may make the dipping sauce up to 1 day before and store it in the fridge.

Cut the leek in half vertically first and then cut it into about 5mm slices. Roughly chop the watercress.

Roughly mix the tempura flour and the ice-cold water using chopsticks in a bowl. Add the calamari, leek and watercress to the batter and combine roughly until all the ingredients are evenly mixed.

Heat the oil in a wok or large frying pan to about 170°C/340°F. If you don't have a thermometer, test the temperature of the oil by dropping a little of the batter into the oil – the batter should touch the base of the pan and float straight back to the surface after 5 seconds. If the batter stays at the bottom of the pan for a while, the temperature is too low. If the batter jumps right back that means it's too high.

Use 2 tablespoons to scoop and then slide the calamari, leek and watercress mixture into the hot oil. Make sure not to overcrowd the pan. Turn the tempura over from time to time and cook for 1–2 minutes, depending on the thickness of each one. Remove using a slotted spoon and drain on kitchen paper. Serve the tempura with a small bowl of the ponzu sauce on the side for dipping.

HORSE MACKEREL AND ONION PATTIES

A traditional fisherman's dish from Chiba prefecture. It's rustic and tastes of the sea.

SERVES 4 (MAKES 12)

400g skinless horse mackerel or mackerel fillets
½ teaspoon salt
1 large onion, finely chopped
2 tablespoons koji miso paste
1 teaspoon finely grated ginger
½ teaspoon instant dashi powder
12–16 shiso leaves
4 tablespoons vegetable, corn or sunflower oil
2 limes, cut into wedges, to serve
seven-spice powder, to serve

Wash the mackerel fillets and pat dry with kitchen paper. Make sure all the bones have been removed. Sprinkle the salt over the fish fillets and leave them for 5 minutes.

Rinse the salt off the fish, and pat the fillets dry with kitchen paper. Chop finely on a large chopping board, or use a food processor but take care not to over-blitz the fish to a paste. Add the onion to the chopping board with the fish, and chop together until very fine and well-combined. Transfer the mixture to a bowl.

Add the miso paste, ginger and dashi powder to the bowl and then mix well. Take a small handful of mixture and make a half-moon shaped patty and then flatten. Repeat with the remaining mixture until you have about 12 patties.

Wrap each patty in a shiso leaf, making sure the jagged edges of the leaves are pointing toward the top, or the curved edge, of the patty.

Heat the oil in a frying pan over medium heat. Once the oil is smoking hot, turn the heat down to low, add the patties and fry, in batches, for about 3 minutes. Turn over and cook the other side for a further 2–3 minutes.

Serve with lime wedges and seven-spice powder on the side.

MISO ARANCINI

Japanese people love rice. This is a great example of Japan meets Italy:
Japanese ingredients cooked the Italian way. It works!

MAKES 24

450g short-grain white rice

4 tablespoons koji miso paste

2 teaspoons mirin

1 teaspoon instant dashi powder

100g chestnut mushrooms, finely
chopped

1 leek, finely chopped

3 eggs

handful of basil leaves

100g mozzarella, cut into small cubes

1 litre vegetable or sunflower oil, for
deep-frying

150–200g panko breadcrumbs

3–4 tablespoons wasabi mayonnaise
(page 47), optional, to serve

1 tablespoon sweet chilli sauce
mixed with 3–4 tablespoons crème
fraîche, optional, to serve

Wash the rice, put it in a saucepan with 500ml water and soak for at least 30 minutes and up to 2 hours.

Loosen the miso paste with the mirin by stirring them together in a small bowl. Add the dashi powder and mix well.

Add the chopped mushrooms, leek and miso mixture to the pan with the rice and the water. Cook the rice as per the instructions on page 29 (alternatively, use a rice cooker).

When the rice is cooked, turn off the heat and leave it to sit with the lid on for 10–15 minutes, then stir and transfer to a large shallow dish. Spread the rice mixture to form an even layer, then leave to cool to room temperature. Beat 1 egg, add this to the rice and combine well.

Form ping-pong sized balls and press your thumb into each ball half way to make an indentation. Push a basil leaf and a cube of mozzarella into the indentation then mould the rice mixture around to seal. Make sure the mozzarella is completely covered and incased in the rice. Place the balls on a plate and cover with cling film. Chill in the fridge for 15 minutes, to firm up.

Heat the oil in a wok or a large frying pan to 180°C/350°F. Beat the remaining 2 eggs and scatter the breadcrumbs on a plate. Dip each rice ball into the egg first, then into the breadcrumbs to coat. Carefully drop the balls, in batches, into the hot oil. Deep-fry for about 2 minutes, or until the balls are golden. Remove with a slotted spoon and leave them to drain on kitchen paper for 2 minutes. Serve the arancini with wasabi mayonnaise and/or chilli crème fraîche.

CRISP-FRIED SHISO AVOCADO

Wrapped in shiso leaves and fried may seem like an unconventional way to eat avocado, but it works. A healthy and light vegetarian dish, yet rich and creamy.

SERVES 4

2 avocados
juice of 1 lime
20g dried wakame seaweed
100g panko breadcrumbs
130g buckwheat flour
½ teaspoon salt
½ teaspoon ground black pepper
1 egg
vegetable or sunflower oil, for deep-frying
12 shiso leaves
12 purple chicory leaves, to serve

For the wasabi mayonnaise
200ml Japanese or good-quality mayonnaise
1 tablespoon soy sauce
1–2 teaspoons wasabi paste, or freshly grated wasabi

Cut the avocados in half and then peel the skin off. Remove the stone from each avocado, and slice the flesh into 6 pieces. Put in a bowl and squeeze the lime juice over the top (this will prevent them from discolouring).

Lightly crush the dried wakame seaweed into smaller pieces, then mix together with the panko breadcrumbs in a shallow bowl. Next, season the flour with salt and pepper on a plate and beat the egg in a bowl.

Pour enough oil to come up to 2.5cm in a small frying pan and heat it to about 170°C/340°F.

Combine the mayonnaise, soy sauce and wasabi in a small bowl and set aside.

Wrap a piece of avocado with a shiso leaf and then dust with the seasoned flour, holding the shiso leaf in place. Dip into the beaten egg followed by the wakame breadcrumbs, and gently press the breadcrumbs onto the shiso-wrapped avocado to coat.

Once the oil is hot, carefully drop in the crumbed avocado pieces and deep-fry until light golden brown. Remove with a slotted spoon and serve each shiso avocado on a purple chicory leaf. Have the wasabi mayonnaise on the side for dipping.

JAPANESE PADRON PEPPERS

I love, love, love this simple side dish. Padron peppers are one of many popular Spanish tapas dishes and here I've given you the Japanese version.

SERVES 4

25–30 large padron peppers
1 tablespoon vegetable, corn or
    sunflower oil
1 teaspoon sesame oil
125ml dashi stock (page 28) or ½
    teaspoon instant dashi powder
    mixed with water
2 tablespoons soy sauce
3 tablespoons mirin
3 tablespoons sake
10g fine bonito flakes
3 tablespoons sesame seeds

Bring plenty of water to the boil in a large saucepan. Add the peppers and cook for 1 minute. Drain well in a colander and then shake off as much excess water as possible.

Heat both oils in a frying pan over high heat. Add the drained peppers and stir-fry them for about 2 minutes. Add the dashi stock, soy sauce, mirin, sake and bonito flakes, then turn down the heat to medium-low. Simmer for 3–4 minutes, or until all the liquid has evaporated and the peppers are soft.

In a separate small frying pan, add the sesame seeds and slowly dry-toast them by shaking the pan until the seeds start to colour and make a cracking sound. As soon as you hear them crack, turn off the heat, tip the seeds on top of the peppers and then mix well.

Serve hot or at room temperature. This dish can be made a few days in advance, kept in the fridge and bought to room temperature before serving.

EDAMAME
AND TOFU DIP

Silken tofu is the perfect ingredient for dips, creating a rich taste and
creamy texture. This recipe is a good example of a successful vegan dish
that doesn't compromise on taste.

SERVES 4

300g silken tofu
1 tablespoon salt
500g frozen edamame beans, shell on
1 teaspoon instant dashi powder
2 tablespoons mirin
25–35g miso paste
1 teaspoon yuzu kosho (yuzu pepper
    paste)
3–4 tablespoons sunflower oil
2 teaspoons roasted sesame oil, for
    drizzling
1 tablespoon chopped chives, to
    serve
1 tablespoon toasted sesame seeds
salt and freshly ground black pepper

Cut the tofu into large cubes. To remove its water content, bring a small
saucepan of water to the boil, add the tofu and blanch for 2–3 minutes. Drain in
a colander and leave to cool for 5 minutes.

Bring plenty of water to the boil in a large saucepan with the salt over very high
heat. Add the frozen edamame, bring back to the boil and then cook for 2–3
minutes. Drain and rinse the edamame beans under cold running water for 30
seconds then put them in a bowl of ice-cold water. This process will help the
beans to retain their bright green colour. Pop the edamame beans out from their
pods.

Mix the dashi powder with mirin and miso paste in a small bowl until
well combined.

Add the edamame beans, cooled silken tofu, miso and dashi mixture, yuzu
kosho and half of the sunflower oil to a food processor and blitz. Slowly pour
in the rest of the oil, little by little, taking care the mixture doesn't become too
runny, and blitz until you have a smooth texture that is firm enough for a dip.
Season with salt and pepper to taste and transfer to a bowl.

Chill the dip in the fridge for at least 1 hour and up to 48 hours. To serve,
drizzle a little roasted sesame oil on top and sprinkle with the chopped chives
and sesame seeds.

RICE

This section will focus upon rice: a renowned staple of the Japanese diet, with its cultivation very much part of Japanese culture and paddy fields covering much of the countryside. The Japanese will only consume Japanese rice as it is said that foreign rice tastes bad – still, rice actually came to Japan from China, in the third century Middle Yayoi period. It is used to produce wine, rice cakes, sweets, snacks, sauces, soy products and vinegar.

Although as a starchy carbohydrate rice would not be recommended in most modern weight-loss focused 'diets', the consumption of this natural grain maintains blood sugar levels and encourages low consumption of processed carbohydrates. In fact, the Japanese equivalent to a lunchtime sandwich is *onigiri*: rice filled with vegetables, seaweeds, seafood or meat and wrapped in seaweed, therefore containing no dairy or gluten, with bread replaced by a natural grain and a sea-vegetable superfood.

While *onigiri* stands in for a sandwich lunch, the Japanese equivalent of the great British fry-up or American pancakes is a breakfast consisting of rice, miso soup, grilled fish, pickles and possibly a *tamago-yaki* egg roll. This is considered a treat, yet it is an incredibly healthy way to start the day – free from added sugars, gluten and dairy, and full of protein and vitamins. In this way, a healthy diet is part of an engrained, centuries-old Japanese lifestyle. That said, toast and cereals with coffee or tea are increasingly eaten in Japan like everywhere else in the world.

GRILLED SALMON AND RICE SOUP

Salmon and seaweed are a match made in heaven, and a fantastic encapsulation of the sea in a bowl.

SERVES 4

110g short-grain brown rice
2 salmon fillets (wild salmon is preferred for its lower fat content and bright orange hue), about 160g per fillet
2 teaspoons table salt
12g dried wakame seaweed, crushed
2 tablespoons toasted white sesame seeds
6–8 shiso leaves, finely sliced
1 tablespoon roasted sesame oil

For the pickled vegetables
½ cucumber
½ Chinese cabbage or white cabbage
1 small carrot
420ml cold water
2 tablespoons salt (for rubbing on the vegetables), plus 1 teaspoon
5g dried wakame seaweed
a pinch of dried chilli flakes
2 teaspoons instant dashi powder

For the broth
1 litre dashi stock (page 28) or 2 teaspoons instant dashi powder mixed with water
1 teaspoon soy sauce
2 teaspoons mirin
good-quality sea salt, to season

First prepare the pickled vegetables. Cut the cucumber and cabbage into small bite-size pieces and slice the carrot into short, thin strips. Mix all the vegetables together in a bowl and add 200ml of the water and 2 tablespoons salt. Rub and squeeze all the ingredients in the bowl together for about 5 minutes or until the vegetables become a little tender but are still crunchy.

Drain the water from the vegetables, then rinse the vegetables thoroughly and squeeze all the water out completely.

Place the vegetable mixture, wakame, chilli flakes, dashi powder, remaining 1 teaspoon salt and remaining 220ml water in a bowl and mix together well. Cover and chill the pickled vegetable mixture for at least 2 hours before serving. Store in an airtight container in the fridge for up to 3 days. Drain lightly before serving.

Next wash the rice and soak it in plenty of water for at least 30 minutes and up to 2 hours. Place in a saucepan with 750ml water and cook the rice according to the instructions on page 29, increasing the cooking time to 30 minutes until the rice is tender to bite.

Sprinkle the salmon fillets with the table salt and leave to cure in the fridge for 30 minutes to 1 hour. Pat them dry with kitchen paper and heat a griddle pan over medium-high heat. Grill the salmon for 3–4 minutes, skin-side down, turn over and grill skin-side up for a further 3–4 minutes, taking care the skin is crisp not burnt. When the salmon is cooked, let it cool enough to handle, then take the skin off and flake.

As soon as the rice is cooked, turn off the heat and sprinkle the rice with the crushed dried wakame seaweed. Replace the lid and let it sit for about 15 minutes.

Heat the dashi stock in a saucepan and stir in the soy sauce and mirin. Season with a pinch of sea salt, keeping in mind the cured salmon will add saltiness.

Mix the toasted sesame seeds into the rice, then scoop into individual shallow bowls. Place the flaked salmon on top of the rice and then pour the hot broth into the bowl. Sprinkle with finely sliced shiso leaves and then drizzle a little sesame oil on top. Serve with crunchy pickled vegetables.

TUNA TARTARE RICE

Tuna sashimi lovers must try this dish. As long as you obtain good-quality fresh tuna, it's the easiest dish to create. Using a ready-made Japanese mayonnaise will make this even less of a hassle to put together.

SERVES 4

150g daikon radish, peeled and cut into thin matchsticks

1 tablespoon salt

12 shiso leaves or a handful watercress

300g sashimi-quality tuna

1 bunch of spring onions, finely chopped

1 tablespoon roasted sesame oil

1 tablespoon soy sauce, plus extra to serve

450g freshly cooked rice (page 29)

4 nori sheets

wasabi mayonnaise (page 47), to serve

Transfer the daikon radish to a bowl, add the salt and rub into the daikon. (The salt will draw out the water from daikon.) Rinse well under cold running water to get rid of the salt and drain in a colander. Cut the shiso leaves thinly and then toss well with the daikon. Set aside.

Chop half the tuna very finely until minced and roughly chop the other half to keep some texture. Put in a medium to large bowl with the chopped spring onions. Season with sesame oil and soy sauce and mix gently.

Leave the freshly cooked rice to come to room temperature. Scoop two handful of rice into individual bowls. Quickly tear the nori sheets into small pieces and sprinkle over the rice. Place the daikon and shiso mixture over the nori followed by the tuna mixture on top. Lastly, add a big dollop of wasabi mayonnaise in the centre. Serve with extra soy sauce and wasabi on the side.

WILD JAPANESE MUSHROOM RICE

This creation is my ultimate favourite rice dish. The secret ingredient is anchovy. Those of you who claim they don't like anchovy, in this dish I insist!

SERVES 4–6

2 tablespoons good-quality olive oil

1 leek, finely sliced

1 garlic clove, finely sliced

½ teaspoon dried chilli flakes

4–6 tinned anchovy fillets, roughly chopped (or kombu sprinkles)

300g mixed Japanese mushrooms (enoki, shiitake, shimeji)

2 tablespoons white wine

450g cooked brown short-grain rice, cold

1 teaspoon instant dashi powder (or kombu dashi powder)

15g unsalted butter

1 tablespoon soy sauce

pinch of ground white pepper

4 heaped tablespoons chopped flat-leaf parsley

2 nori sheets

½ lemon, cut into wedges, to serve

Heat olive oil in a wok or very large frying pan over medium-high heat. Add the leek and the garlic, and stir-fry for about 1 minute.

Add the chilli flakes, anchovy fillets and the mushrooms to the pan and cook for 1 minute. Pour in the wine and turn the heat up to high to burn off the alcohol, shaking the pan for about 1 minute.

Turn the heat down to medium, then add the cooked rice and dashi powder to the pan. Fry together mixing everything well, then add the butter and soy sauce. Finally, season with white pepper and turn off the heat. Add the parsley and mix through gently.

Place the nori sheets directly over a gas flame until very crisp and slightly charred. Alternatively, put the nori sheets in a single layer on a baking tray and toast under the grill, turning every 10 seconds to prevent burning.

Portion the rice into individual bowls. Shred the nori with both hands and sprinkle over the rice and serve with the lemon wedges on the side.

UNAGI EEL DONBURI

Once upon a time, *unagi* was a dish frequently eaten and enjoyed in Japanese homes. And rightly so, as it is rich and tasty as well as being highly nutritious. However, due to the massive decline in eel populations in recent years, it is now a luxury dish.

SERVES 4

450g short-grain rice
4 eggs
1 teaspoon instant dashi powder
125ml mirin, plus 1 tablespoon
3–4 fillets pre-cooked unagi (eel)
125ml soy sauce
3 tablespoons sake
4 tablespoons sugar
1 bunch of spring onions, finely sliced
   on the diagonal
sansho pepper, to serve

Rinse the rice and cook according to the instructions on page 29.

Crack the eggs into a bowl and whisk well with the dashi powder and 1 tablespoon mirin. Heat a small frying pan with a little vegetable oil over high heat. Pour one quarter of the egg mixture into the pan, tilting to spread the eggs evenly in the pan. The eggs will cook almost immediately; flip over and cook the other side. When done, take the omelette out and place on a chopping board. Repeat 3 more times to get 4 crêpe-like eggs. Set aside.

Preheat the grill to high. Open the unagi packet and remove the whole fillets. Lay them, skin-side down, on a lightly oiled grill rack. Grill for 1 minute and then turn over and grill for a further 2–3 minutes, or until the skin just starts to char. Take them out of the grill immediately and leave to sit for about 2 minutes on a chopping board to slightly cool. Cut the unagi into about 1cm-thick slices.

In a small saucepan, combine the soy sauce, sake, sugar and 125ml mirin. Over medium heat bring to the boil and simmer for 2–3 minutes, until the sauce becomes thicker and like single cream in consistency.

Cut the omelettes into thin ribbons and then mix with the spring onions in a bowl.

Pour half of the sauce over the steaming hot rice and mix, then scoop into individual bowls or lacquer (or plastic) square containers. Scatter the egg and spring onion mixture over the rice. Lay sliced unagi randomly on top, drizzle the rest of the sauce over the unagi and serve immediately with sansho pepper on the side.

CALAMARI STUFFED WITH STICKY RICE

Ika meshi is a very traditional dish, which hails from Hokkaido in the northern island of Japan, known for the best quality squid, in abundance. You can find this delicious squid in bento boxes at train stations all over Japan – the perfect kind of fast food.

SERVES 4

420g glutinous rice or risotto rice
2 medium dried shiitake mushrooms
2 tablespoons sugar, plus 1 teaspoon
400g calamari (approx. 4 whole
   medium-large calamari)
250ml sake
125ml soy sauce
125ml mirin
30g ginger, peeled and sliced, plus
   extra for serving

Rinse the sticky rice a couple of times and then drain in a colander. Put the dried shiitake mushrooms in a bowl with 500ml warm water and 1 teaspoon sugar. Leave both of them to sit for about 1 hour.

Unless you've bought ready-prepared calamari, you will need to prepare the calamari. Pull out the tentacles from the body by holding the body tight. Remove the quill and organs from inside the body. Cut off the head making sure to remove the sharp beak between the head and tentacles. Slice the core part of tentacles into 2–4 pieces. Rinse thoroughly.

Squeeze the excess water from the mushrooms, keeping the soaking liquid aside, and then chop the mushrooms finely. Mix the rice and chopped mushrooms in a bowl and then stuff into the calamari, filling only 60 per cent and then securing with a toothpick.

In a wok or frying pan, add the mushroom soaking liquid, sake, soy sauce, mirin, 2 tablespoons sugar, sliced ginger and 800ml water. Arrange the stuffed calamari in the pan laying them in a single layer. Flatten each calamari pocket using the back of a spoon to ensure the rice is evenly spread inside. Place the tentacles around the edge and bring to the boil over high heat.

Once it reaches the boil, skim the scum off the surface, taking care not to remove the cooking liquid. Turn the heat down to medium-low and place a sheet of parchment paper or foil on top of the calamari. Simmer for about 30 minutes, making sure the calamari is submerged in the liquid at all times.

Carefully remove the parchment and use tongs to take the calamari out of the pan. Keep them covered, so that they don't dry out. Turn up the heat to medium-high and simmer to reduce the cooking liquid to one-third, or until it becomes a syrupy consistency.

Cut the calamari into about 1cm thick slices using a sharp knife. Assemble the stuffed and sliced calamari with the tentacles on the side on a plate. Pour the thick sauce over the calamari and serve with extra thinly sliced ginger if you like. This dish can be served at room temperature or just warm.

PRAWN AND TOFU ON RICE

I created this surprisingly good dish using 'things in the fridge' for lunch and it worked so well. A light and healthy one-bowl dish.

SERVES 4

450g short-grain rice
300g firm tofu, roughly chopped into bite-sized pieces
400g raw prawns, deshelled and deveined
2 tablespoons vegetable oil
1 bunch of spring onions, finely chopped
30g ginger, peeled and grated
2 tablespoons roasted sesame oil
½ teaspoon salt
½ teaspoon ground white pepper
handful of coriander leaves, roughly chopped

For the sauce
60g miso paste
2 tablespoons oyster sauce
1–2 teaspoons chilli paste
120ml mirin
2 tablespoons sake
1 teaspoon cornflour

Rinse the rice and cook as per the instructions on page 29.

Wrap the chopped tofu in kitchen paper and place a chopping board on top along with some weights (such as a couple of tin of beans to help weigh down the board). Leave to drain for about 30 minutes, then, using your hands, squeeze the excess water from the wrapped tofu. Unravel and crumble the tofu, then set aside.

Chop the prawns into small pieces by hand, keeping the texture a bit rough. Set aside.

For the sauce mix all the ingredients in a small bowl, until there are no lumps of flour. Set aside.

Heat the vegetable oil in a wok or a large frying pan over medium heat, add the spring onions and grated ginger, and stir-fry for about 2 minutes.

Add the crumbled tofu and sesame oil, and then season with the salt and pepper. Continue to stir-fry for 3–4 minutes, until the crumbled tofu has coloured a little and liquid evaporated.

Turn the heat up to high, add the chopped prawns and stir-fry for 1 minute. Once the prawns begin to turn pink, pour in the sauce mixture and continue to stir-fry over high heat for about 2 minutes.

Scoop the cooked rice into bowls and then put the tofu and prawn mixture on top of the rice. If you like, pour some of the sauce from the pan over the rice too, then finish with the coriander to decorate.

AUTUMN RICE

This is a beautifully subtle vegan dish. Because it can be difficult to obtain fresh bamboo shoots, I'm adding a selection of mushrooms that combine to enhance the autumnal flavours.

SERVES 4

450g brown short-grain rice

625ml vegetarian stock (page 28), at room temperature

50g dried shiitake mushrooms

pinch of sugar

50g shimeji mushrooms

150g cooked bamboo shoot (tinned or vacuum packed), rinsed and thinly sliced

2 teaspoons yuzu kosho (yuzu pepper paste)

1½ tablespoons soy sauce

3 tablespoons mirin

1 tablespoon sake

100g edamame beans

1 tablespoon roasted sesame oil

1 tablespoon black sesame seeds

sea salt

Wash the rice well and then place in a pan with the vegetarian stock. Leave to soak for at least 30 minutes. Soak the dried shiitake mushrooms in a bowl of warm water with a pinch of sugar for at least 30 minutes (the sugar will make the mushrooms plumper).

Drain the shiitake mushrooms, trim off the stalks and cut the caps into thin slices. Trim the root part from the shimeji mushrooms and the tear them into bite-sized chunks. Add all the mushrooms and the bamboo shoot to the pan with the rice.

Mix the yuzu kosho, soy sauce, mirin and sake in a bowl. Pour this seasoning mixture into the pan with the rice. Place over high heat, cover and bring to the boil. Turn the heat down and let it simmer, covered, for about 15 minutes. Turn off the heat and then leave it to sit for a further 15 minutes.

While the rice cooks, bring a pan of water and 1 teaspoon salt to the boil. Add the edamame beans and blanch for 5 minutes, until just cooked. Drain and rinse under cold running water to cool and help retain the bright green colour.

Remove the edamame beans from their pods and mix into the rice and mushrooms until well combined. Check for seasoning and add sesame oil, salt and/or more yuzu kosho to taste. Serve in bowls with a sprinkling of black sesame seeds.

HIJIKI SEAWEED RICE

Detox food can be so tasty. When you're in need of a little cleanse after eating red meat, dairy or oily food, try this dish. It really is absolutely tasty, and nourishing.

SERVES 4

450g short-grain brown rice
40g dried hijiki seaweed
80g shimeji mushrooms
2 sheets *aburaage* (Japanese deep-
    fried tofu)
1 tablespoon roasted sesame oil
2 tablespoons vegetable, sunflower
    or corn oil
2 medium carrots, cut into
    matchsticks
125ml dashi stock (page 28), or 1
    teaspoon instant dashi powder
    mixed with water
2 tablespoons mirin
3 tablespoons soy sauce
1 teaspoon sugar
100g pickled daikon radish, thinly
    sliced
2 tablespoons toasted white sesame
    seeds
salt

Wash the rice and soak it in plenty of water for at least 30 minutes and up to 2 hours. Put the rice in a saucepan with 900ml water and cook on high heat for 5 minutes. Once the water begins to boil reduce the heat and simmer for 25–30 minutes. Remove from the heat and keep warm.

Soak the hijiki in a bowl of water for about 30 minutes. Drain through a colander and then rinse a few times. Leave them in the colander to dry.

Trim the tough root part of the mushrooms and then separate the stalks from the caps.

Rinse the *aburaage* sheets by pouring over just-boiled water and then letting it cool slightly. Squeeze out the water and then thinly slice.

Heat both the oils in a wok or large frying pan, add the carrots and stir-fry them for about 1 minute over high heat. Then add the hijiki and mushrooms along with a pinch of salt. Fry quickly for a further minute, pour in the dashi stock, mirin, soy sauce and sprinkle in the sugar. Turn the heat down to low and simmer, stirring all the time, until almost all of the liquid has evaporated. Throw in the *aburaage*, give everything one more stir, then turn off the heat (the *aburaage* will soak up any remaining liquid).

Take the pan off the heat and scoop the vegetable and aburaage mixture into a large mixing bowl along with the rice. Add the pickled daikon radish, sesame seeds and then mix well until combined. Serve in individual bowls or in a large bowl as you like.

JAPANESE MISO RISOTTO

This is the perfect breakfast the morning after a heavy night of drinking or when you might be feeling a little under the weather. The key is to cook the egg yolks runny; the oozing yolk and miso make a heavenly combination.

SERVES 4

1 litre vegetarian stock (page 28)
450g cold, cooked short-grain rice
¼ savoy cabbage, chopped
1 courgette, chopped
2 spring onions, finely chopped
200g shiitake mushrooms, thinly sliced
2 tablespoons miso paste
2 tablespoons white miso paste
4 free-range organic eggs
handful of watercress leaves, to garnish
shichimi togarashi, to serve

Heat the vegetarian stock in a medium saucepan (a wide and shallow pan is ideal) and bring to the boil. Add the cooked rice and stir, making sure there are no lumps of rice stuck together. Add the cabbage, courgette, spring onions and mushrooms and bring back to the boil over high heat. Turn the heat down to low and simmer for 5–6 minutes.

Dissolve both the miso pastes with 2–3 tablespoons hot water in a small bowl. Add this mixture to the pan, stirring well.

Use the back of a ladle to make 4 wells on the surface of the rice and then crack the eggs on top, making sure each egg is well apart and retains its shape. Put the lid on and continue to simmer for 2 minutes, or until the whites are done but the yolks still runny.

Serve the risotto in individual bowls with one egg each. Sprinkle the watercress around the egg and serve with shichimi togarashi on the side.

SUPER VEGAN DONBURI

When I create a delicious, super healthy dish, it is so satisfying. This is
exactly that kind of dish. It's beautiful, delicious and vegan.

SERVES 4

335g brown short-grain rice
30g dried arame or hijiki seaweed
2 tablespoons vegetable oil
200g lotus roots, peeled and thinly
   sliced
200g okra, cut into 1cm pieces
1 teaspoon yuzu kosho (yuzu pepper
   paste)
4 tablespoons soy sauce
2 tablespoons mirin
2 teaspoons rice vinegar
1 tablespoon sugar
1 tablespoon cornflour, mixed with 1
   tablespoon water
2 tablespoons sesame oil

Wash the rice thoroughly and soak it in a bowl of water for 30 minutes. Cook
for about 30 minutes, or following the instructions on the packet.

Meanwhile, soak the arame seaweed in a bowl of warm water for 10 minutes.
Drain and set aside in a colander to drain.

Heat the oil in a large frying pan or wok and stir-fry the lotus roots over high
heat for 2 minutes. Turn the heat down to medium and the add the arame and
okra. Add the yuzu-kosho, soy sauce, mirin, rice vinegar and sugar, then turn
the heat down to low and cook for a further 3 minutes.

Turn the heat up to medium-high, pour in the cornflour-water mixture and stir
until everything is combined and the sauce slightly thickened. Turn off the heat,
drizzle over the sesame oil and quickly stir.

Pour the whole mixture over the cooked brown rice in a bowl and serve.

NOODLES

Soba are the most popular of all of the noodle varieties available in Japan, and during our hot, heady summers, we often have cold soba with dipping sauces (made from a base of dashi stock and mirin), and add seaweed, wasabi and spring onion to taste.

Made from buckwheat, soba noodles are the healthiest type of noodle too. While living in Hong Kong with my husband, where my children were born, I developed a taste for Chinese and Western food and put on a fair bit of weight during each of my pregnancies. When my children were aged one and three, we moved to Tokyo and I suddenly became very aware of my weight as Japanese women are so slim, and I no longer was! Still, I didn't want to go on an unhealthily drastic diet, so every day for three months I ate a lunch of cold soba noodles with grated daikon, wasabi and seaweed – which I thoroughly enjoyed. Within three months I had lost ten kilos, and reached a weight that I have maintained on a mainly Japanese diet ever since.

As well as soba noodles, there are udon, somen, shirataki, *hiyamugi* and ramen – all of which are cooked in a pot of boiling water until *al dente*. Although the egg-based ramen noodles originate from China, and are perhaps the least traditional of our noodles, they are now very popular. Ramen joints have popped up all over Japanese cities where various hot dishes are served with dark soy sauce, miso, *tonkotsu* (pork) or with steaming gyoza dumplings, and cold ramen are heaped with mounds of raw vegetables.

RAMEN NOODLES WITH PORK BROTH AND CHAR-SIU PORK

I can't have a noodle chapter in the book without including a recipe for *tonkotsu* ramen. It's the fastest growing in popularity of Japanese dishes right now. The key to achieving great ramen is to source the right ingredients, and cook the broth for long enough.

SERVES 4

For the ramen stock
1.5kg pork shoulder, with bone in or ribs (or 500g chicken drumsticks or wings)
100g ginger, peeled and roughly sliced
2 leeks
1 large onion, peeled and quartered
4 garlic cloves, bruised
1 cabbage, core only
2 carrots, cut into chunks
15g dried kombu
250ml sake
1 teaspoon salt
1 teaspoon freshly ground black pepper

For the char-siu pork
600g boneless pork belly
vegetable oil, for frying
5cm piece ginger, peeled and sliced
3–4 spring onions, cut into 5cm lengths
4 tablespoons mirin
120–160ml soy sauce
2 tablespoons caster sugar

For the tonkotsu broth
1.2 litres ramen stock (see above)
2 tablespoons mirin
1 tablespoon soy sauce
250ml char-siu pork broth (see above)
1–2 tablespoons tahini paste
salt and ground white pepper

To serve
300g fresh ramen egg noodles (if you can't find fresh ramen noodles you could use fresh spaghetti)
handful of beansprouts
120g jar of menma (fermented bamboo shoots)
4 hard-boiled eggs, peeled and cut in half lengthways
2 handfuls of finely chopped spring onions, green part only
1 tablespoon toasted white sesame seeds
ground white pepper
rah-yu, chilli-infused sesame oil, or roasted sesame oil and chilli paste

First make the ramen stock. Preheat the oven to 240°C/475°F/Gas Mark 9. Bruise or bash the pork bones with the back of a knife or meat tenderiser. Put them in a roasting tin and bake in the oven for about 20 minutes, until the bones are lightly browned. Alternatively, brown them in a dry frying pan for 5–6 minutes over high heat.

Bring 4 litres water to the boil in a large saucepan. Put the pork in the pan and cook for 15–30 minutes, skimming the scum off the surface from time to time. Add 2 litres water along with the remaining ingredients for the stock, and simmer for at least 5–6 hours and up to 24 hours with the lid on. Check from time to time and top up with more water if necessary.

Recipe continued on page 74

Strain the stock through a colander lined with a muslin cloth. It's best to leave it to drain, which will take about an hour (alternatively, squeeze the muslin very gently and occasionally as the stock is being strained). When most of the ingredients in the colander become quite dry, discard them. Transfer the stock to an airtight container and store in the fridge (this can be made up to 3–4 days in advance, it can also be stored in the freezer for up to about 3 months).

To make the char-siu pork, cut the pork into 2 chunks and heat oil in a wok or large frying pan over high heat until smoking. Add the pork belly and brown, skin-side facing up, until caramelised.

Fill a large saucepan with 1 litre water and bring to the boil over high heat. Add the pork belly, ginger and spring onions, and boil rapidly for 10 minutes. Skim off any scum that rises to the surface. Turn the heat down to low and simmer gently for about 1 hour, covered, making sure the pork is submerged at all times and topping up with extra water if necessary.

Add the mirin, soy sauce and sugar, and simmer for a further 45 minutes. Turn off the heat and allow the pork to steep and cool down in the broth.

Once cooled, transfer the pork out of the broth into an airtight container and keep in the fridge. This can easily be made a few days in advance if you prefer. Keep the stock from the pork for using in other dishes and measure out 250ml for use later in this recipe and set aside.

When almost ready to serve, remove the pork from the fridge and slice into 12 pieces. Allow to come to room temperature while you prepare all your toppings.

Next, heat all the ingredients for the tonkotsu ramen broth except the tahini paste in a large saucepan and bring to the boil. Turn down the heat and simmer for 10 minutes. While the broth is simmering, scoop up a small amount of liquid from the pan into a small bowl and then stir in the tahini paste until smooth. Pour this mixture back into the broth and stir well.

Bring plenty of water to the boil in a saucepan and cook the noodles for about 2 minutes, or follow the instructions on the packet. Heat a small pan with a dash of oil and fry the beansprouts for 2 minutes.

Divide the hot noodles between 4 individual noodle bowls. Pour some broth into each bowl, dividing it evenly between the bowls. Lay the slices of cha-siu pork, menma and boiled egg halves on top of the noodles. Finally, add the beansprouts, sprinkle over the spring onions, sesame seeds, white pepper and drizzle with the chilli-infused sesame oil (or serve with the sesame oil and the chilli paste for people to add their own).

SHIRATAKI NOODLES WITH CHUKA SAUCE

Shirataki, slippery yam noodles, are known as one of the best diet ingredients because they contain zero calories. They have a unique texture – springy, gelatinous and chewy – but don't have a lot of flavour, making them ideal for soaking up the robust depths of the *chuka* sauce.

SERVES 4

400g shirataki noodles
2 tablespoons vegetable, corn or
    sunflower oil
40g ginger, peeled and finely chopped
4 spring onions, finely chopped
150g minced pork
1 yellow pepper, finely sliced
1 courgette, finely sliced
1 red chilli, finely sliced
200g raw prawns, deshelled and
    deveined
1 bunch of coriander, leaves and
    stalks separated and roughly
    chopped
4 tablespoons toasted sesame seeds

For the chuka sauce
1 teaspoon instant dashi powder
2 tablespoons soy sauce
1 tablespoon oyster sauce
1 tablespoon sake
1 tablespoon sugar
2 tablespoons toasted sesame oil

First rinse the shirataki noodles well in cold water and then drain in a colander. Spread the noodles on a large chopping board and then cut them to easy-to-eat noodle lengths (these noodles are often sold very long).

Mix all the sauce ingredients in a bowl, then set aside.

In a large wok, heat the oil over medium heat, add the ginger and spring onions, then stir-fry for about 30 seconds. Add the pork, yellow pepper, courgette and chilli, and continue to stir-fry for 1–2 minutes, until the pork is a light brown.

Add the prawns and the coriander stalks, and cook for a further 1–2 minutes or until the prawns are just cooked. Turn up the heat to high and add the shirataki noodles and chuka sauce. Cook, tossing and mixing, for another 1–2 minutes, or until most of the liquid has evaporated.

Take off the heat, add the sesame seeds and give everything a final toss. Transfer to one large bowl to share and sprinkle with the coriander leaves.

SEARED DUCK BREAST SOBA IN BROTH

Duck is the absolute perfect meat for this dish, its richness embuing the broth with a deeper, full flavour. Remember to keep the duck skin. Hands-down this is one of my favourite ways to enjoy traditional soba noodles.

SERVES 4

600g duck breasts
2 teaspoons yuzu kosho (yuzu pepper paste)
2 litres dashi stock (page 28)
4–6 tablespoons soy sauce
4 tablespoons mirin
2 tablespoons sake
pinch of salt
320–400g dried soba noodles
2 bunches of spring onions, finely chopped
¼ daikon radish, approx. 75g, grated
shichimi togarashi and/or sansho pepper, to serve

Prepare the duck breasts first by carefully trimming off the sinew. Make sure to pluck any hairs in the skin or use a blowtorch to burn them off.

Spread the yuzu kosho over the flesh side of the duck and leave them for about 5 minutes.

Heat a frying pan over medium-high heat and place the duck breasts skin-side down. Almost immediately after touching the heat you will see the fat coming out. Remain cooking for about 2–3 minutes.

Turn the heat down to medium-low, flip the duck over to sear the other side for about 2 minutes and then brown the sides. Turn the duck skin-side down again, reduce the heat to low, cover loosely with foil and leave to cook for 2–3 minutes, or until cooked to your preference. Once they are cooked, take them out and leave them to rest for at least 5 minutes.

While the duck breasts are resting, make the soup. Heat the dashi stock in a saucepan and then add the soy sauce, mirin and sake. Bring to the boil, turn the heat down and simmer for about 3 minutes. Taste and season with salt and/or soy sauce if necessary.

Bring a pan of water to the boil and cook the soba noodles for 4–5 minutes or follow the instructions on the packet.

Once the duck breasts have rested, slice them into about 5mm-thick slices. Quickly drain the soba noodles and portion out into individual noodle bowls. Pour the broth over the noodles, lay the sliced duck on top followed by a handful of finely chopped spring onions. Finally, add a spoonful of grated daikon radish to finish. Serve immediately with shichimi togarashi and/or sansho pepper.

BANG BANG CHICKEN WITH SOMEN NOODLES

Steamed chicken breast, silky somen noodles and a rich sesame sauce make a sensational trio, ideal for a summer lunch.

SERVES 4

4 dried shiitake mushrooms
2 large skinless chicken breasts or
    4 small skinless chicken breasts
2cm piece of ginger, peeled and thinly
    sliced
4 spring onions, roughly chopped
½ teaspoon salt
4 tablespoons sake
handful of salad leaves
200g somen noodles
½ cucumber, cut into fine matchsticks

For the sesame sauce
2 tablespoons soy sauce
2 tablespoons mirin
3 tablespoons tahini paste
3 tablespoons black sesame seeds,
    ground

For the deep-fried onions
250ml oil, for deep-frying
¼ onion or 2 shallots, thinly sliced
    (alternatively, you can buy
    ready-fried shallots in Chinese
    supermarkets)

Soak the dried shiitake mushrooms in a bowl with 250ml boiling water for 20 minutes. Drain and reserve 4 tablespoons of the mushroom soaking water.

Preheat the oven to 250°C/480°F/Gas Mark 8. Line a roasting tray with a generous amount of foil and place the chicken breasts, ginger, shiitake mushrooms and spring onions on top. Sprinkle with the salt, then fold the foil up and around to make a parcel. Seal all but one of the edges tightly, then pour the sake and the mushroom-soaked water into the gap in the parcel. Seal the last edge tightly and cook in the oven for 20–30 minutes, depending on the size of the chicken breasts, until the chicken is cooked.

Take the parcel out of the tray and leave the chicken to cool inside the parcel.

Meanwhile, make the sesame sauce by mixing all the ingredients except for the ground sesame seeds in a small bowl until smooth and very thick.

Next prepare the deep-fried onions. Heat the oil in a large frying pan and deep-fry the onion or shallots until beginning to turn golden and crispy. Remove with a slotted spoon and drain on kitchen paper.

Rinse the salad leaves in very cold water to refresh them and chop or tear them into bite-size pieces.

Bring plenty of water to the boil in a large pan and cook the somen noodles for about 2 minutes. Drain, rinse well in cold water and set aside to drain completely in a colander.

Once the chicken has cooled to room temperature, remove from the parcel and shred or thinly slice. Add 3–4 tablespoons of the chicken cooking juices from the parcel to the sesame sauce along with the ground black sesame seeds and stir together. If the consistency is too thick, add more of the chicken cooking juices.

Place the noodles on individual plates followed by the chicken. Pour over the sauce, garnish with the salad leaves and cucumber, and scatter with a few deep-fried onions.

UDON NOODLES WITH CURRY SAUCE

Since katsu curry is so popular and in such high demand in the UK, I'm introducing another traditional curry dish. Silky and elastic udon noodles are perfect in this dish, mopping up the creamy curry sauce.

SERVES 4

10g butter

1 tablespoon vegetable oil

1½ large onions, finely chopped

1 medium carrot, grated

200g minced chicken thigh

1 tablespoon curry powder

1 litre dashi stock (page 28) or 2 teaspoons instant dashi powder mixed with water

100ml soy sauce

250ml semi-skimmed milk or soy milk

1 teaspoon sugar

½ teaspoon salt

2 teaspoons mango chutney

320g dried udon noodles

4 tablespoons finely chopped spring onions

In a large saucepan, heat the butter and vegetable oil very gently. Once the butter melts, add the onions and sauté gently for about 2 minutes. Add the grated carrot and keep sautéing gently for 25–30 minutes, or until the onions are caramelised.

Add the minced chicken and curry powder and cook, stirring until the chicken changes colour, for about 2 minutes. Slowly pour the stock into the pan, stirring all the time, and bring to the boil. Add the soy sauce, milk or soy milk, sugar and salt. Turn down the heat and simmer for about 20 minutes then stir in the mango chutney.

While the curry is simmering, prepare the noodles. Fill a large saucepan with plenty of water and bring to the boil. Add the noodles and cook over high heat for 7–10 minutes, or according to the packet instructions. Drain well in a colander and then portion into 4 bowls.

Ladle the piping hot curry sauce over the udon, sprinkle with chopped spring onions and serve immediately.

SOBA NOODLE ROLLS WITH NORI SHEET

A very pretty and alternative way of serving soba noodles, this dish treats the noodles like sushi rice to create a variety of rolls. I've introduced two types by using ordinary and green tea soba noodles.

MAKES 8 ROLLS, 4 OF EACH TYPE

100–120g dried soba noodles
100–120g dried cha soba noodles
8 nori sheets
220ml noodle broth (page 29)
wasabi paste

For the cha soba roll filling
4 tablespoons wasabi mayonnaise (page 47)
4 spring onions, finely chopped
⅓ cucumber, deseeded and cut into matchsticks
8–12 tempura prawns (see the recipe on page 201 but replace the crab with prawns)

For the plain soba roll filling
1 roasted red pepper, sliced
40g soft cheese, such as brie or camembert
8 cooked asparagus spears, or green beans
40g pickled ginger, squeezed of excess moisture and roughly chopped
2 teaspoons wasabi paste

In a large pan, bring plenty of water to the boil and add the plain soba noodles. Cook for 4–5 minutes or according to the packet instructions. Drain under running cold water and rinse until the soba is cold and then leave the noodles in the colander. Repeat with the cha soba noodles.

Prepare all the fillings and have them ready on the work surface. Divide the noodles into 4 portions for each plain soba and cha soba noodles.

Place a bamboo sushi mat on the work surface with a nori sheet on top, making sure the rough side of the sheet is facing up and the shiny side is down.

First, make the cha soba rolls. Pick up small bundle of cha soba noodles, grabbing them as if squeezing water out from the top to the bottom. Place the bundle across the nori sheet from left to right, making sure the noodles are long enough to reach end to end. Spread the noodles up and down the sheet until two-thirds of the sheet is covered, leaving the top one-third uncovered. Trim the ends of the noodles and discard.

In the centre of the soba, spread 1 tablespoon of wasabi mayonnaise, across from left to right, in a 3cm line and then sprinkle the chopped spring onions to cover the mayonnaise. Add a few cucumber sticks and a couple of prawns making sure the prawn tails stick out at the edge of the nori (you may need three prawns per roll).

Using the sushi mat as a guide, roll the nori around the noodles and the filling, gently pressing and tightening as you roll. The end part of the nori sheet is not secure at this point but do not dab it with water otherwise the nori will disintegrate. Simply leave the nori with the overlapping side down and let the natural moisture from the noodles stick the nori together. Repeat the filling and rolling for the remaining rolls until you have 4 of each type.

Slice the rolls, diagonally or straight, into 6–8 pieces using a very sharp knife. Serve with noodle broth and wasabi paste.

JAPANESE SAVOURY PANCAKE

Japanese pancake or bubble and squeak? This is such a satisfying dish as it has everything in it and is so scrumptious! My version is in the simpler Kansai style, whereas the Hiroshima style includes egg noodles in the batter mix. The condiments are very important and tonkatsu sauce is a definite must.

SERVES 4

420g plain flour
4 eggs, beaten
½ teaspoon baking powder
3 teaspoons instant dashi powder
1 pointed cabbage, shredded
2 bunches of spring onions, finely
   chopped
1½ tablespoons vegetable oil, for
   frying
2 tablespoons tenkasu or deep-fried
   shallots (page 79 or available from
   Chinese supermarkets)

Optional toppings
prawns, calamari, thinly sliced pork
   belly or beef, sweetcorn, halloumi
   cheese, as you like

**For the tonkatsu sauce (makes
about 180ml)**
3 tablespoons Worcestershire sauce
2 tablespoons soy sauce
2 tablespoons caster sugar
5 tablespoons tomato ketchup
1 tablespoon sake
½–1 teaspoon English mustard

To serve
mayonnaise or mustard, optional
2 tablespoons ao-nori (seaweed)
   powder
20g bonito flakes

First make the tonkatsu sauce. Put all the ingredients, except the mustard, in a small saucepan. Bring to the boil, then reduce the heat and simmer, uncovered, for about 7 minutes or until the mixture is thickened to the consistency of tomato ketchup. Remove from the heat and cool, then stir in the mustard to taste. Refrigerate and use as required.

Put the flour in a large bowl, add 500ml water and mix. Once all the flour has been combined with the water, add the beaten eggs, baking powder and dashi powder then mix well until the batter is smooth with no lumps.

Add the cabbage and spring onions and mix in well. This is the base of the *okonomi-yaki* pancake.

Heat a little oil in a large frying pan over medium heat. When hot, pour the pancake mixture into the pan, tilting the pan to spread the mixture out to a thickness of about 1.5cm. Sprinkle with deep-fried shallots and your choice of toppings, making sure to evenly spread them over the surface of the whole pancake.

Reduce the heat to low and partially cover with a lid (to release the condensation) and cook for about 15 minutes depending on the size of the pancake, making sure the bottom of the pancake is not burnt.

Flip the pancake over, using two large spatulas, and then cook for a further 5 minutes without the lid until done. To check if the pancake is cooked, insert a toothpick into the centre and it should come out dry. If the toothpick comes out with sticky batter attached, flip it over again and leave it to cook for a few more minutes.

Transfer the pancake onto a large plate and then slather with the tonkatsu sauce, mayonnaise and mustard if you like. Sprinkle with ao-nori and bonito flakes to finish.

YAKISOBA WITH FRIED EGG

Although Japan is not known for its streetfood culture, we have a few typical street festival foods. Yakisoba is one of them. The addition of fried egg gives an extra joy to this dish. For a vegetarian option, use smoked tofu in place of the chicken.

SERVES 4

200g calamari
200g boneless and skinless chicken thighs
2 tablespoons vegetable, corn or sunflower oil
1 large onion, thinly sliced
2 medium carrots, thinly sliced
1 green pepper, thinly sliced
¼ savoy cabbage, roughly chopped
pinch of salt and ground white pepper
200g cooked egg noodles
2 tablespoons Worcestershire sauce
120ml tonkatsu sauce (page 84)
½ teaspoon roasted sesame oil
4 eggs
2 tablespoons ao-nori (seaweed) powder, to serve
2 tablespoons deep-fried shallots (page 79 or use shop-bought), to serve

Prepare the calamari. Peel away the skin and wash under cold running water, pull the main bone out, then wash the inside again. Cut into bite-sized pieces. If you can obtain tentacles, they will give a nice texture and appearance. Cut the chicken thighs into similar bite-sized chunks.

Heat 1 tablespoon oil in a large wok or frying pan over medium-high heat and then add the onion. Fry the onion for 1 minute and then add the rest of the vegetables and chicken. Season with salt and white pepper and stir-fry for 3 minutes, or until all the chicken is cooked and the vegetables still have a little crunch.

Turn up the heat and add the calamari. Stir-fry and toss for about 1 minute, or until the calamari is just cooked.

Add about 2 teaspoons oil to the noodles to prevent them from sticking then add them to the pan. Pour in the Worcestershire and tonkatsu sauces and keep stir-frying for another 1–2 minutes, mixing well and tossing all the time. Turn the heat off.

In a separate frying pan, heat the sesame oil and 1 teaspoon oil over medium heat and then crack all 4 eggs into the pan. Cover with a lid, turn the heat down to medium-low and fry for about 1 minute. Then take the lid off and cook the eggs to the level you like. (I prefer runny egg yolks and cooked whites.)

Divide the stir-fried noodles, chicken and vegetables between individual plates or bowls and then top each with a fried egg. Sprinkle with ao-nori and deep-fried shallots.

UDON NOODLES WITH ENOKI MUSHROOMS AND ARAME SEAWEED

This very traditional udon is served simply with thick ankake broth, ginger and sometimes spring onions. Although I have added a few extra elements to this dish, it is still in keeping with the traditional flavour, which comes from our core ingredients of soy sauce, mirin, sake and ginger, which gives the dish its distinctive flavour profile.

SERVES 4

200g dried udon noodles
50g dried arame seaweed
200g enoki mushrooms
80g mangetout
1 tablespoon cornflour mixed with 2
    tablespoons water
1 courgette, spiralised or sliced into
    very fine strips
60g ginger, peeled and grated or very
    thinly sliced

For the ankake broth
1 litre vegetarian stock (page 28)
2 tablespoons mirin
2 tablespoons soy sauce
1 tablespoon sake
½ teaspoon sea salt

Bring plenty of water to the boil in a large pan and cook the udon noodles for 9–10 minutes, or follow the instructions on the packet. At the same time soak the dried arame in water for about 10 minutes.

Meanwhile, trim the enoki mushrooms and then separate the stalks from the caps. Set aside.

Blanch the mangetout in a pan of slightly salted water for about 1 minute, then drain and rinse under cold water until cooled. Slice the mangetout thinly and set aside.

Next make the ankake broth. Heat the vegetarian stock in a large saucepan with the mirin, soy sauce, sake and sea salt. Once it comes to the boil, add the mushrooms and arame and then cook for 2–3 minutes.

Pour the cornflour mixture into the pan, stirring well, and let it boil for a couple of minutes until the broth thickens.

Add the courgettes to the pan and simmer for 1–2 minutes, put in the noodles in the final moments and then use a slotted spoon to transfer to a colander.

Divide the courgette and udon noodles between 4 individual bowls and then pour the thick stock mixture over the top. Sprinkle the slices of mangetout and ginger sparingly on top and serve hot.

SOBA NOODLES WITH BROCCOLI PESTO

This dish has to be one of my top five new recipes. Melting broccoli, pine nuts and miso make a perfect, rich Japanese pesto. This can be served either cold or hot; both are utterly delicious!

SERVES 4

600g broccoli
1 teaspoon salt
2 tablespoons toasted pine nuts
120ml olive oil, plus extra if needed
50g miso paste
4 tablespoons mirin
60g ginger, grated
2 garlic cloves, grated
1 teaspoon good-quality sea salt
1–2 fresh red chillies, very finely
   chopped, optional
280g dried soba noodles
handful of watercress, to serve

To make the broccoli pesto, cut the stem part of the broccoli to separate it from the florets. Chop the stem into 1cm cubes and then cut the florets into small bite-sized pieces.

Bring plenty of water to the boil in a large saucepan with 1 teaspoon salt, add the broccoli stems and blanch for 2 minutes. Add the florets and boil for 5 minutes. Drain and rinse under cold running water until the broccoli has cooled. Drain well.

Put the broccoli, toasted pine nuts, olive oil, miso paste, mirin, grated ginger and garlic and good-quality sea salt in a food processor and blitz for 1 minute leaving a little bit of texture.

If using the chilli, stir this into the pesto rather than blitzing it in a food processor (this will help keep the vibrant green of the broccoli).

Bring a pan of water to the boil and cook the soba noodles for about 4 minutes, or according to the instructions on the packet, until *al dente*.

If you are serving this hot, cook the noodles for about 1 minute less than the instructions suggest. Drain and rinse well under hot water, then return the noodles to the pan along with the pesto. Heat for 30 seconds. If it becomes too dry, add a little more olive oil.

If you are serving this cold, drain the noodles in a colander and rinse briefly under cold water. Transfer to a large bowl with the pesto and toss together well. Serve with a little watercress on top.

WHITE MISO SPAGHETTI CARBONARA

The sweetness and creaminess of white miso works perfectly in a carbonara-style sauce and it also helps balance the saltiness. It is utterly delicious. Make sure to use sweet white miso for this dish, as although it's usually more expensive the cheaper versions can be too salty.

SERVES 4

400g dried spaghetti (plain or brown)
100g pancetta
240g shiimeji mushrooms
2 whole eggs, plus 2 egg yolks
120g sweet white miso
2 tablespoons mirin
100g Parmesan cheese, grated
handful of chives, chopped, to serve
salt and freshly ground black pepper

Bring a large pan of water to the boil (you will need at least 4 litres for this amount of pasta). Add 1 teaspoon salt, then throw in the pasta and cook for 10 minutes, or according to packet instructions.

While the pasta is cooking, dice the pancetta and trim the shimeji mushrooms then break them up into bite-sized pieces. Heat a frying pan and fry the pancetta and shimeji for only a couple minutes without any oil (the pancetta will render its fats).

In a bowl, mix the whole eggs and yolks with the white miso and mirin and grated Parmesan until well combined. There may still be lumps of miso at this point, but these will melt in once tossed with the hot pasta.

Check the pasta is *al dente* and then immediately take the pan off the heat and drain the pasta. Throw the pasta back into the pan along with the pancetta and mushrooms, and mix well. Add the egg and miso mixture and then toss well, making sure the pasta is not sticking and everything is tossed properly. (Do this off the heat otherwise your eggs will scramble.)

Season to taste with freshly ground black pepper, if necessary. Lightly toss the whole thing again and then divide between individual pasta bowls. Serve immediately with a sprinkling of chopped chives.

FISH AND SHELLFISH

The Japanese population consumes more fish than any nation in the world – 85g daily on average – while maintaining one of the highest life expectancies in the world. We eat a great deal of oily fish, whose omega-3 fatty acids aid in a healthy heart and brain and are said to prevent joint problems, allowing for an active lifestyle into old age. Contrary to popular belief, sashimi is generally eaten on special occasions as part of a meal, and the majority of fish dishes are cooked. The Japanese don't eat raw fish all of the time.

While Japanese markets are famous for their fish, what I really marvel at and miss is the quality of the fish available at Japanese supermarkets. Beautiful whole fish take up an enormous expanse, with a vast selection of sashimi, clams, prawns and local seafood – all freshly brought in that morning and filleted for all different ways of cooking. I'm glad that fresh fish are now far more readily available in the UK, but frozen seafood works as a great alternative.

In Japan, we value all types of fish and use each in very different ways. Currently, my favourite fish is sea bream and I adore it lightly cured and infused with kombu seaweed (the recipe is on page 104).

BLOWTORCHED PICKLED MACKEREL

Pickled mackerel, known as *Shime-Saba*, is a very traditional method of cooking mackerel for using in sushi. Blowtorching the fish intensifies its flavour while softening the fish, making it meltingly delicious.

SERVES 4

2 teaspoons salt

4 fresh mackerel fillets, with skin on

10g dried wakame seaweed

80g pickled ginger, thinly sliced, including pickling liquid

2 teaspoons sesame seeds

1 tablespoon ao-nori (seaweed) powder

1 lime, cut into wedges, to serve

salt and pepper

For the pickling liquid

200ml rice vinegar

1 tablespoon soy sauce

2 tablespoons sugar

½ teaspoon black peppercorns

½ onion, thinly sliced

For the fennel

2 large fennel bulbs

75ml olive oil

Mix all the ingredients for the pickling liquid in a saucepan and heat gently. Bring to a boil and simmer for few minutes. Let it cool completely then store in the fridge (this will keep in the fridge for a few days if making in advance).

For the mackerel, sprinkle the salt over the fish fillets and leave for about 10 minutes. The salt will draw water out from the mackerel. Pat the mackerel dry with kitchen paper, place in a shallow dish and then pour the cooled pickling liquid over. Cover with cling film and leave to pickle for 2–3 hours somewhere cool or in the fridge.

About 30 minutes before cooking, take the mackerel fillets out of the pickling liquid.

Preheat the oven to 200°C/400°F/Gas Mark 6. Cut off the top part of fennel and keep the fine thin leaves for the garnish. First, cut the fennel in half, then thinly slice it vertically, from the stalk end to the base. In a large baking tray, pour in half the olive oil, lay the sliced fennel on top and then pour over the rest of the olive oil. Season with salt and pepper and cover with foil. Cook for about 12 minutes then remove from the oven. Turn the fennel slices over and return to the oven to cook, uncovered, for a further 5–7 minutes, or until soft and slightly caramelised. Take the fennel out of the tray to cool and set aside, and reserve the oil in the tray.

Soak the wakame in a bowl of water for about 10 minutes. Drain and squeeze any excess water from the wakame. Chop the wakame and put it in the tray with the oil reserved from the fennel along with the pickled ginger. Toss together.

Pat the mackerel fillets dry with kitchen paper and cut each fillet, lengthwise, into 2; you should have 8 pieces. Keep the pickling liquid.

Lay the mackerel fillets, skin-side down, on an oven tray rack. Using a blowtorch, start by grilling the flesh side of each fillet, then turn the fillets over and char the skin – it needs to be slightly burnt to achieve the charcoal flavour.

To serve, place the fennel on the plate first, criss-cross 2 mackerel pieces on top then add the wakame and ginger. Finally, garnish with the reserved fine fennel leaves and sprinkle the ao-nori powder over the whole plate. Serve slightly warm with lime wedges on the side.

SARDINES WITH UMEBOSHI

Traditionally, this dish is best eaten in summer to provide energy to get through hot summer days. Sardine is not only the most nutrient-dense fish, full of omega-3 and vitamins, but it is also flavoursome. The tanginess of umeboshi goes hand in hand with the sardines.

SERVES 4

8 fresh sardines, cleaned, heads removed
2 tablespoons soy sauce
4 tablespoons mirin
2 tablespoons sake
1 teaspoon sugar
30g ginger, peeled and sliced, plus 20g cut into very fine matchsticks
8 medium-sized umeboshi (you can buy them online or in Japanese supermarkets)

Rinse the sardines well under cold running water.

In a saucepan large enough to accommodate the sardines in a single layer or a deep frying pan, add the soy sauce, mirin, sake, sugar, sliced ginger and 300ml water. Place over medium heat and bring to the boil. Once boiling, lay all the sardines on the bottom of the pan and then carefully slot the umeboshi into the gaps between the sardines.

Cook over medium heat for 10–12 minutes with the lid on, then turn off the heat.

Carefully remove the sardines and umeboshi from the pan and lay them on a serving plate. Put the pan back over high heat and boil the cooking juices for a few minutes until reduced by about 20 per cent – the sauce should be a slightly syrupy consistency.

To serve, spoon the sauce over the sardines and umeboshi. To finish, place the finely sliced ginger on top of the sardines.

YELLOWTAIL SASHIMI WITH YUZU AND TRUFFLE DRESSING

Try this dish for a smart dinner party – I promise it will be a hit. It's also very easy and stress-free to prepare. The yellowtail sashimi and truffle oil offer a real sense of luxury.

SERVES 4

400g sashimi-quality yellowtail
2 ripe passion fruit
handful of chives
200g watercress, optional

For the yuzu dressing
4 shallots, very finely chopped
3 tablespoons yuzu juice
2 tablespoons rice vinegar
½ teaspoon instant dashi powder
1 tablespoon soft brown sugar
1 tablespoon truffle oil

First, make the yuzu dressing. Combine all the ingredients for the dressing in a bowl at least 30 minutes before serving. You may keep this for 2 days in the fridge, however if you are not serving it on the same day, add the truffle oil at the last minute.

Use a very sharp knife to cut the yellowtail into thin sashimi slices, about 3mm thick (see Note below).

Halve the passion fruit and scrape the flesh and seeds out. Make sure to loosen the flesh slightly if a bit lumpy.

Arrange the yellowtail slices prettily on a plate. Draw a line using the passion fruit in the middle of the line of the fish, and drizzle over the yuzu dressing. Finally, sprinkle with chives. If you wanted, you could serve this with a mound of watercress on the side.

Note: Sashimi must be sliced against the grain using a very sharp, long-bladed knife. Short knives are not suitable because you need to make too many motions per slice. If you have sharp long blade, one stroke will cut the piece. This way you have a clean, mirror-surface smooth slice of fish.

TUNA TATAKI WITH AVOCADO MOUSSE

Tuna is no longer an unusual dish, perhaps because it is easy to cook and so tasty. Rich and creamy avocado goes extremely well with lean fish like tuna and the tangy sourness of umeboshi.

SERVES 4

4 tablespoons black sesame seeds

4 tablespoons white sesame seeds

1 tablespoon vegetable or sunflower oil

400g sashimi-quality tuna

2 large ripe plums

250ml cooking oil, for deep-frying

4 nori sheets

For the umeboshi dressing

2 tablespoons umeboshi purée (or 2 large umeboshi, destoned and flesh puréed)

1 onion, grated

4 tablespoons rice vinegar

1 tablespoon soy sauce

4 tablespoons mirin

1 tablespoon sugar

2 tablespoons vegetable or sunflower oil

For the avocado mousse

1 shallot

1 garlic clove

2 ripe avocados

handful of rocket, or watercress or coriander leaves

1 shallot, roughly chopped

1 garlic clove, peeled

juice of 1 lime

4 tablespoons olive oil

pinch of salt

2 tablespoons plain non-fat yoghurt, optional

Mix together all the ingredients for the umeboshi dressing. Make this at least 30 minutes before serving and keep it in the fridge until needed.

Prepare the tuna. Mix the black and white sesame seeds in a small bowl. Lay a large sheet of cling film out on a clean work surface. Spread half of the mixed sesame seeds over the cling film. Brush the vegetable or sunflower oil all over the surface of the tuna and then dip it in the sesame seeds. Cover the top part of tuna with the remaining sesame seeds and press the tuna lightly to help the seeds stick. Fold over the cling film to encase the tuna and wrap firmly. Keep in the fridge for at least 30 minutes.

While the dressing and tuna are cooling in the fridge, prepare the avocado mousse. Using either a food processor or a stick blender, blitz the shallot and garlic until fine. Add the remaining ingredients except the yoghurt and blitz until it has a smooth texture. If you like the texture and flavour as is, there is no need to add the yoghurt. If you want a lighter taste or if it's too thick, stir through the yoghurt. Set aside until ready to serve.

Take the tuna out of the fridge and unwrap the cling film. Heat a large frying pan over high heat. Place the tuna in the pan and sear 1 side for about 45 seconds. Turn over and sear the other side for the same length of time. Remove the tuna and transfer to a plate and then put it into the fridge to cool.

Peel and cut the plums into small dice. Use a blowtorch to get some caramelisation on the plums. If you don't have a blowtorch then put them under a grill set to the highest heat.

Heat the cooking oil in a small saucepan over medium heat until it reaches 170°C/340°F. Tear each nori sheet into about 5 pieces randomly, drop into the hot oil and quickly deep-fry for 2 seconds. Do not leave them longer otherwise they will burn. Use a slotted spoon to transfer the nori to kitchen paper – they will crisp up instantly.

Take the tuna out of the fridge and cut into 8–10mm thick slices, taking care with the sesame seeds. Spoon or pipe a little avocado mousse diagonally on the plate. Lay the sliced tuna on top of the avocado mousse, scatter the diced plum over the plate and drizzle with the dressing. Lastly, garnish with the nori crisps.

SALMON WINTER SOUP

My all-time favourite soup, this is particularly good in winter. *Sake kasu* is fermented sake lees and has a wonderful sweet aroma that adds an extra dimension to the flavour.

SERVES 4

1 deep-fried tofu sheet

1 teaspoon salt

2 salmon fillets

1.2 litres dashi stock (page 28) or 2½ teaspoons instant dashi powder mixed with water

1 medium carrot, cut into bite-sized pieces

¼ daikon radish, cut into bite-sized pieces

½ leek, sliced on the diagonal

¼ pointed cabbage, sliced

70g sake kasu paste (sake lees)

2 tablespoons miso paste

4 tablespoons mirin

2 tablespoons soy sauce

shichimi togarashi, to serve

Bring a saucepan of water to the boil and blanch the deep-fried tofu sheet for 20 seconds, then drain. When cool enough to handle, squeeze out the excess water and cut the tofu into 1 × 3cm pieces.

Preheat the grill to high. Sprinkle a little salt on both sides of the salmon fillets and then leave them for about 10 minutes to remove any moisture. Pat dry with kitchen paper. Grill the salmon for 2 minutes on each side, until cooked. Remove and allow to cool on a rack.

Bring the dashi to the boil, add the carrot and daikon radish and cook for 3 minutes. Add the leek and cabbage and the cook for a further 3 minutes.

Spoon the sake kasu paste into a bowl, take a ladleful of the hot stock from the pan and pour into the bowl with the sake kasu. Stir to melt until smooth, then return to the pan with the stock and vegetables.

Break the grilled salmon into large bite-sized pieces and add to the pan along with the tofu. Stir in the miso, mirin and soy sauce and taste for seasoning, adjusting the flavour by adding more miso and/or mirin.

Divide between individual bowls and serve the shichimi powder on the side.

BLOWTORCHED SALMON WITH YUZU PONZU DRESSING

One of the top five most popular dishes from my dinner party catering, the richness of the salmon and the zing from yuzu is a delightful match. It's easy to obtain good-quality salmon in the UK now, so get yourself a blowtorch. Hey presto!

SERVES 4

5g dried wakame seaweed
½ tablespoon sesame oil
300g green beans
1 × 480g fresh sashimi-quality salmon
  fillet
100g daikon radish, grated
2 tablespoons sesame seeds

For the yuzu ponzu dressing
2 tablespoons sushi vinegar
3 tablespoons yuzu juice
5 tablespoons soy sauce
1 onion, very finely chopped
½ teaspoon instant kombu dashi
  powder

Mix all ingredients for the yuzu ponzu in a small bowl. Keep it in the fridge for at least 1 hour for the onion to release its sweetness.

Soak the wakame in warm water for 5 minutes, drain and squeeze out excess water. Toss the wakame with sesame oil and set aside.

Quickly boil the green beans in a pan of water until just cooked but retaining the crunchiness, about 3 minutes. Drain and rinse the beans under cold running water until the beans are completely cold. Pat dry and set aside.

Place the salmon fillet on a chopping board and then take the skin off by using a very sharp knife. Cut in half along the central bone of the salmon, then cut the salmon against the grain into 7mm-thick slices.

Line a baking tray with foil and place a grill rack over the top. Lay each salmon piece on the grill rack and use a blowtorch to quickly char the pieces. (This has to be done very quickly otherwise the salmon will cook through.)

Lay a handful of the green beans on a chopping board and trim the ends to ensure they are all exactly the same length. Repeat with the remaining beans. Next, arrange them in line, preferably using a long rectangular plate, forming a neat bed for the salmon fillets to sit on.

To serve, carefully place pieces of salmon on top of the beans, alternating them charred side up and charred side down, giving each person about 6 pieces.

Squeeze the excess moisture from the grated daikon and spoon a line of it onto the salmon. Place the wakame and sesame seeds on top. Serve the yuzu ponzo separately so people can pour on as much of the sauce as they like.

KOMBU-CURED SEA BREAM WITH YUZU PONZU JELLY

Curing fish with kombu is a very authentic Japanese method of preserving fish. Delicate sea bream paired with the subtle flavour of the kombu is just heavenly. This is my ultimate favourite fish dish, and the ponzo jelly is a must have.

SERVES 4

4 sea bream or sea bass fillets, with
    skin on
1 tablespoon sea salt
20g kombu sheets
2 tablespoons sake
4 small shallots
pinch of salt
finely chopped chives, to serve

For the yuzu ponzo jelly
1 gelatine sheet
120ml dashi stock (page 28) or 1
    teaspoon instant dashi powder
    mixed with water
3 tablespoons soy sauce
½ teaspoon fish sauce
1 tablespoon sugar
3–4 tablespoons yuzu juice
2 tablespoons vegetable, sunflower
    or corn oil

Lightly sprinkle the sea bream fillets with sea salt and leave to sit for 5–10 minutes.

Dust off the kombu with a dry tea towel, taking care not to remove all of the white residue from the surface of the kelp. Drizzle the sake over the kombu to moisten and soften. Once softened, cut 2 pieces to a similar size as the fish fillets; keep the rest to one side.

Pat the fish fillets dry with kitchen paper. Place 2 fillets, skin-side down, on a chopping board or a plate and then place 2 pieces of kombu on top of the fish. Place the remaining 2 fish fillets, skin-side up, on top of the kombu, so that the flesh sides of all fillets are facing the kombu. Wrap each sandwich firmly in cling film and chill them in the fridge for 4–6 hours.

Soak the gelatine in a small bowl of cold water for about 10 minutes. Meanwhile, combine the remaining ingredients for the yuzu ponzu jelly in a bowl. Heat the mixture in a small saucepan just to below boiling. Take off the heat. Squeeze the water out of the gelatine and add it to the pan. Mix well, then store in the fridge. This can be heated briefly to warm in a microwave.

About 30 minutes before serving, slice the shallots very finely and soak them in a bowl of cold water with a pinch of salt for 10 minutes. Drain, place in a colander and store in the fridge for 20 minutes.

Unwrap the fish fillets and remove the kombu (keep it to one side for serving), and carefully peel away the skin. Cut them into thin diagonal slices, about 5mm thick. This way of slicing is called 'sogi-giri' in Japanese.

Arrange the kombu used for curing the fish on a serving plate (if it's not large enough use some more sheets), and then top with the sliced sea bream. Drizzle the yuzu ponzo jelly over the sea bream and then sprinkle over the shallots and chopped chives just before serving.

SEA BASS WITH YUZU MISO

One of my favourite Japanese ingredients is white miso. Its versatility lends itself to many dishes, especially seafood and desserts. A perfect match for a delicate fish like sea bass.

SERVES 4

4 large sea bass fillets, with skin on
300g samphire
2 tablespoons vegetable or sunflower oil
½ teaspoon salt
½ teaspoon ground black pepper
4 tablespoons olive oil, or butter
pared zest of 1 lime (or yuzu if available), very finely sliced

For the yuzu miso sauce
80g white miso paste
1 egg yolk
1 whole egg
2 tablespoons mirin
2 tablespoons sake
1 teaspoon sugar
2 teaspoons kombu sprinkles or kombu powder
2–3 tablespoons yuzu juice

Check the sea bass to ensure all the bones are removed. Cut each fillet into large bite-sized pieces, about 4–5 pieces.

Make the yuzu miso sauce. Put the miso paste, egg yolk, whole egg, mirin, sake, sugar and kombu sprinkles in a small saucepan and simmer gently over very low heat, stirring at all times. Be careful not to let the mixture come to the boil otherwise the eggs will scramble – the texture should be silky smooth. Once it reaches just below boiling point, immediately turn off the heat, add the yuzu juice and mix well.

Bring plenty of water to the boil in a medium saucepan. Remove the hard end bits of the samphire as they can be unpleasant to eat. Drop the samphire into the boiling water and cook for a few minutes. Do not add any salt as the samphire is already salty. Drain in a colander and rinse well under ice-cold water. Set aside.

Heat a large frying pan with the vegetable or sunflower oil over medium-high heat. While the pan heats up, season the fish with salt and pepper. Place the fish in the pan, skin-side down, pressing down on the fillets firmly with the back of a fish slice. Cook for about 2 minutes until the skin is crisp. Turn over and drizzle some of the olive oil into the pan and keep drizzling more over the skin while the sea bass cooks, for around 2 minutes.

Divide the samphire between 4 plates, with about 4–5 samphire piles on each plate, followed by a piece of sea bass on top, making sure the crispy skin is facing up. Add a drop of yuzu miso sauce on top, then neatly arrange the finely sliced lime zest on top of the sauce. Finally, drizzle over a little of the oil from the pan the fish was cooked in over the plate.

SOFT PRAWN AND CRAB CAKES

These prawn and crab cakes are incredibly fluffy and light. The ponzo jelly
sauce, with its citrusy zing, cuts through the richness of the seafood.

MAKES 12−16

2 medium potatoes, cut into small
   chunks
4 tablespoons soy milk
120g raw prawns, deveined and tails
   removed
1 tablespoon vegetable or sunflower
   oil, plus extra for deep-frying
1 bunch of spring onions, finely
   chopped
1 teaspoon grated ginger
1½ teaspoons salt
½ teaspoon ground black pepper
2 egg whites
1 teaspoon cornflour
100g crabmeat, brown and white
   meat (1 dressed crab)
4 tablespoons rice flour
70g panko breadcrumbs

To serve
ponzu jelly (page 104)
shichimi togarashi

Bring a pan of water to the boil and add the potatoes and a pinch of salt. Cook
for 12 minutes, until they are just tender. Test to see if they are done by poking a
toothpick into the potato. Drain in a colander and leave them for a few minutes
for any excess water to evaporate.

Using a potato masher or stick blender, purée the potatoes with the soy milk
until smooth but not elastic. Transfer to a large bowl and leave it aside to cool.

Chop the prawns very finely either on a chopping board with a sharp knife or
using a food processor.

Heat 1 tablespoon oil in a frying pan over medium-low heat, add the spring
onions, chopped prawns, ginger and ½ teaspoon each of salt and pepper. Sauté
for about 2 minutes, turn off the heat, then leave it aside to cool.

In a very clean bowl, beat the egg whites with an electric or hand whisk. Add
1 teaspoon salt and the cornflour then whisk again until the egg whites become
quite stiff and can hold their shape.

Add the crabmeat and prawn mixture to a bowl along with the potatoes, and
mix well. Fold in half of the egg whites until combined, then add the remaining
egg whites and gently mix together.

In a small saucepan, pour enough oil to come at least 5cm up the sides. Heat
to about 170°C/340°F. Working quickly, take the prawn and crab mixture and
make small patties. Lightly dredge in rice flour, followed by the breadcrumbs.
Carefully drop the patties, working in batches so as not to overcrowd the pan,
into the hot oil and deep-fry them for 3–4 minutes, or until they become golden
in colour. Remove with a slotted spoon and drain the patties on kitchen paper.

Serve the prawn and crab cakes with ponzu jelly and shichimi togarashi on
the side.

SPICY MISO SOUP WITH PRAWN AND CHICKEN QUENELLES

This is one of my most popular dishes and has been for a long time. If you get bored of plain miso soup with bit of tofu, vegetables or seaweed, try this. The prawn and chicken quenelles provide a nice depth to the broth and the chilli adds a sensational kick.

SERVES 4

100g fresh prawns, deshelled and deveined
100g boneless and skinless chicken breast, cut into chunks
1 egg white, beaten
2 tablespoons chopped spring onions
½ teaspoon grated ginger
½ teaspoon good-quality sea salt
1.5 litres dashi stock (page 28) or 3–4 teaspoons instant dashi powder mixed with water
½ teaspoon chilli paste (or dried chilli or finely chopped fresh chilli)
3 tablespoons miso paste (preferably half red miso and half white miso, mixed)
handful of spinach or watercress leaves

Put the prawns and the chicken in a food processor and mince until you have a smooth paste. Alternatively, mince well with a knife on a chopping board and press the mixture through a sieve until you have a smooth texture. Add the beaten egg white and mix again until combined.

Add the spring onions, ginger and sea salt, and use your hands to mix together well. Set aside.

Bring the stock to the boil in a large saucepan over medium-high heat. Use a tablespoon to scoop some of the prawn and chicken mixture and another tablespoon to form a quenelle shape. Gently drop the quenelle into the stock and repeat until you have used all the prawn and chicken mixture

When the stock comes back to the boil turn the heat down to a simmer and cook the quenelles gently until they all come up to the surface, which should take about 2 minutes. Skim any scum off the surface if necessary.

In a small bowl, mix the chilli and miso pastes. Add a little of the hot stock from the pan and stir until smooth. Then pour the chilli-miso into the pan and stir.

Add the spinach or watercress leaves, immediately turn off the heat and serve.

JAPANESE-STYLE LOBSTER THERMIDOR

Once in a while I want to treat myself with extravagant, indulgent ingredients. Here, the miso and rice vinegar cut through the richness of cream in the sauce. A sensational combination with the succulent lobster.

SERVES 4

2 large or 4 small lobster tails
1.5 litres dashi stock (page 28)
4 baby leeks
fennel tops or cress, to serve

For the creamy white nuta sauce
100g sweet white miso
4 tablespoons soya milk
2 tablespoons double cream
1 tablespoon soy sauce
3 tablespoons mirin
2 tablespoons sushi vinegar
1 egg yolk
1 whole egg
2 teaspoons Dijon mustard
salt and pepper

Clean the lobster and separate the heads and tails. Keep the heads in the freezer for later use (for example a fish soup or bisque). If you can, it would be practical to only purchase the lobster tails for this dish.

Bring the dashi stock to the boil in a large pan. Add the lobster tails to the boiling stock, cover with the lid and boil for 3–4 minutes depending on the size of the lobster. Make sure not to overcook the lobster tails – the flesh should be white and firm but not rubbery. As soon as they are cooked, drain (keep the broth as it is ideal used in fish soup) and keep the lobster tails covered lightly with foil.

In a small saucepan, mix all the white nuta sauce ingredients except for the egg yolk, whole egg and mustard. Heat the mixture very gently and simmer for about 2 minutes, stirring all the time and taking care not to boil. Add the egg yolk and egg and the mustard, then simmer gently for a further 1 minute, stirring all the time, until it reaches the consistency of béchamel sauce. Keep warm and set aside.

In a separate saucepan, bring some water to the boil with a pinch of salt. Holding the green part of the leeks, dip in the white part and cook for about 1 minute, then drop the whole leeks in for a further 1 minute. Drain and squeeze the excess water from the leeks, then pat dry. Cut the leeks into pieces about 2cm thick and then mix them into the white nuta sauce. Keep warm.

Cut the inside centre of the lobster tail, remove the little legs, making sure that the whole shell is not broken as it will be used to serve. Take the lobster flesh out from the shells and cut it into bite-sized pieces. Toss the lobster pieces with half of the white nuta sauce and then equally divide them between the shells. Pour the remaining miso mixture on top of the lobster.

Preheat the grill to medium-high heat. Place the lobsters on a grill rack and then grill for about 2 minutes or until the top turns light golden in colour. Sprinkle the fine fennel leaves on top and serve.

MISO SCALLOP WITH EDAMAME PURÉE

This is a Japanese version of the classic, scallops with pea purée. By using Japanese flavourings, the dish takes on a different dimension. It's light yet there is richness from miso and edamame.

SERVES 3–4

2 garlic cloves, grated

50g miso paste

3 tablespoons mirin

1 teaspoon sugar

1 teaspoon Dijon mustard

vegetable oil, for frying

12 medium fresh scallops (white part only)

½ teaspoon salt

½ teaspoon ground black pepper

handful of fine fennel leaves, to garnish

For the edamame purée

1 teaspoon salt

500g frozen edamame beans, shell on

120ml dashi stock (page 28) or 1 teaspoon instant dashi powder mixed with water

1 tablespoon mirin

1 teaspoon soy sauce

Make the edamame purée. In a very large saucepan, bring plenty of water and the salt to the boil over high heat. Rinse the frozen edamame under hot water from a tap in a colander to give them a good start at defrosting. Add the edamame into the pan of boiling water and cook for about 3 minutes.

Drain the edamame under cold running water for 30 seconds then put them in a bowl of ice-cold water for a few minutes. (This will keep the bright green colour of edamame beans.) Pod the beans.

Heat the dashi stock, mirin and soy sauce in a saucepan and simmer for 2 minutes, then turn off the heat and cool.

Add the edamame and about half of the stock to a food processor and blitz. Check the consistency and then blitz again, adding the remaining dashi mixture little by little taking care it doesn't become too runny. Blitz until it reaches a purée or slightly rough texture as preferred. Keep warm and set aside.

To cook the scallops, mix the grated garlic, miso paste, mirin, sugar, Dijon mustard and 2 tablespoons water in a small bowl until smooth. This mixture should be quite runny.

Heat a large frying pan with a little vegetable oil over medium-high heat. Add the scallops to the pan, season with the salt and pepper and quickly sear for 1–1½ minutes on each side, depending on the size of the scallops, until nicely golden and slightly crisp at the edges. The inside of the scallops should still be a little raw at this point.

Pour the miso mixture into the pan and cook the scallops for a further 30 seconds on each side, over medium-high heat, turning the scallops and using them to mop up the miso mixture. Turn off the heat, remove the scallops from the pan and place on kitchen towel to prevent further cooking.

To serve, place the edamame purée on plates and then place the scallops on top. If the scallops are large, cut them in half horizontally to make them easy to eat. Sprinkle the fine fennel leaves on top.

MEAT AND POULTRY

Any history of food in Japan has to include the many centuries when eating the meat of four-legged animals was forbidden. For more than a thousand years prior to 1868 there was a strict ban, initiated by Buddhist beliefs. Interestingly, the eating of wild boar and hare was tolerated, which perhaps contributes to the fact that pork remains, today, the most commonly used meat in Japan. As the country modernised in the late 19th century, meat eating was encouraged as part of a process of Westernisation. However, as eating meat was never originally rooted in Japanese food culture, it is still eaten in relatively small quantities.

These days the Japanese diet continues to rely mainly on rice, vegetable and tofu-based dishes, and this limited consumption of red meat is thought to be behind the long lifespans and slim waistlines of the Japanese population. Beef in particular can still be very expensive in Japan, so when it is included in a dish, it is the star of the dish, rather than just an ingredient.

This is consistent with the well-known Japanese adage 'eat until you are 80 per cent full', which is much easier to do when tasting many contrasting dishes, rather than dining on a single heavy meat dish.

As Japan is surrounded by sea, it is not surprising that we continue to make the most out of what is readily available in terms of protein, while much of our farmland is dedicated to rice paddies.

SWEET GINGER MEATBALLS

Here is another traditional Japanese-Western dish. Meatballs may not sound Japanese but it's all about the sauce. Try these for a different angle on meatballs.

SERVES 4

1 bunch of spring onions, finely chopped
250g minced beef
250g minced pork
20g grated ginger
1 egg
2 teaspoons roasted sesame oil
1 tablespoon cornflour, plus extra for dusting
vegetable, sunflower or corn oil, for shallow frying
1 tablespoon white sesame seeds
salt and ground white pepper

For the sweet ginger sauce
30g grated ginger
3 tablespoons soy sauce
125ml dashi stock (page 28) or 1 teaspoon instant dashi powder mixed with water
2 tablespoons sugar
3 tablespoons mirin
3 tablespoons rice vinegar
1 teaspoon cornflour

Put the chopped spring onions (reserve a handful of the green part for the garnish) in a bowl with the beef and pork mince, grated ginger, egg, sesame oil and pinch of salt and white pepper. Start adding the cornflour, little by little, kneading the mixture well for a few minutes until doughy and elastic.

Scoop portions of the meat mixture with a teaspoon to make bite-sized balls. Make sure all the meatballs are the same size to ensure consistent cooking times. Dust them lightly in cornflour.

Pour enough oil to come up to about 1cm deep in a large frying pan and set over medium heat. Once the oil reaches about 160°C/320°F, drop the meatballs carefully into the pan. Shallow-fry them by turning them in the oil until they are just cooked, 3–4 minutes depending on the size of the meatballs. Alternatively, for a healthier option, bake the meatballs with a drizzle of oil in an oven preheated to 180°C/350°F/Gas Mark 4 for 12–15 minutes.

While the meatballs are cooking, squeeze the juice from the grated ginger into a small bowl along with the other ingredients for the sauce and mix well until there are no lumps.

Heat a large frying pan and add the cooked meatballs. Once the pan becomes very hot, pour in the sauce mixture, shake the pan from side to side to coat the meatballs well and let the sauce thicken, about 1 minute. Transfer to large shallow bowls, sprinkle with the finely chopped spring onion greens and finish with the toasted sesame seeds sprinkled on the top.

MISO APPLE PORK BELLY

Pork and apple is a match made in heaven. The sweetness of apple and saltiness of miso gives almost a savoury salted caramel effect for this meltingly soft pork belly.

SERVES 4

1kg pork belly
1 fennel bulb, finely sliced, including fennel fronds
½ teaspoon salt
3 tablespoons rice vinegar
1 teaspoon Dijon mustard
1 teaspoon sugar
1 red chilli, finely chopped

For the marinade

100g red or koji miso paste
4 tablespoons mirin
2 tablespoons sake
2 tablespoons sugar
4–5 spring onions, finely chopped
1 apple, grated
20g grated ginger, optional

Score the pork belly skin using a sharp knife, in a criss-cross pattern, to absorb the marinade.

Put the miso, mirin, sake and sugar in a bowl and mix well.

Lay the pork belly on large tray, skin-side down, and pour about 70 per cent of the marinade over the pork. (Keep the reserved marinade in a container or bowl.) Rub the pork belly with the marinade, making sure it is well coated all over, then leave it to marinate for 24 hours. If you don't have enough time to marinate it, cut the pork belly into thinner chunks and rub the marinade all over each chunk of pork belly well.

Sprinkle the sliced fennel with salt and rub in until the fennel softens a little. Briefly rinse off the salt and then combine with the vinegar, mustard and sugar in a bowl. Lightly pickle for about 30 minutes. This can be kept in the fridge for up to 2 days.

Preheat the oven to 180°C/350°F/Gas Mark 4. Take the pork out of the marinade and use kitchen paper to wipe the pork to rid it of excess marinade (this will prevent the outside from burning before the pork is cooked through). Pour the reserved marinade into the container or bowl with the rest of the marinade and save for later. Place the pork, skin-side up on a wire rack set over a deep roasting tray, half filled with just-boiled water.

Cook in the oven for about 30 minutes, turn the heat down to 140°C/275°F/Gas Mark 1 and then continue to cook for a further 3 hours or until the pork is meltingly tender. Keep an eye on the water level during cooking and top up with fresh hot water from time to time. Once the pork is done, remove from the oven and then cut it into chunks.

Put the reserved marinade in a small saucepan with the spring onions and apple. Simmer for 3–4 minutes and then add the grated ginger if you like. The liquid will reduce to the consistency of thick chutney.

To serve, lightly squeeze excess liquid from the fennel slices and arrange on serving plates. Place the pork on top of the fennel, sprinkle with fine fennel leaves and finely chopped chilli and finish with a drop of miso chutney alongside the pork.

PORK, CALAMARI AND GREEN BEANS IN SPICY SOY-MAYO

This is one of the quickest and tastiest midweek dinners. It can be served with plain rice or in a *donburi* style. One dish has it all … meat, seafood and vegetables.

SERVES 4

200g green beans, trimmed
2 tablespoons vegetable oil
1 leek, finely chopped
2 garlic cloves, finely chopped
200g thinly sliced pork belly
120g calamari, cleaned and cut into
   1cm rings (or use frozen)
handful of coriander leaves
salt

For the spicy soy-mayo sauce
3 tablespoons soy sauce
2 tablespoons sake
2 tablespoons mirin
2–3 teaspoons sugar
4 tablespoons mayonnaise
1 tablespoon sesame oil
½ teaspoon cornflour
1–2 teaspoons chilli bean paste

To make the spicy soy-mayo sauce, whisk the ingredients in a bowl with 1 tablespoon water and set aside.

Bring a pan of water to the boil with a pinch of salt and blanch the green beans for about 3 minutes, drain under cold water until the beans are cool and set aside.

Heat the vegetable oil in a large frying pan or wok over medium heat. Fry the leek and garlic for 30 seconds, turn up the heat to high and stir in the pork and calamari. Stir-fry for 1 minute, or until both the pork and calamari are just about cooked.

Add the green beans and stir-fry for 1 minute. Pour the soy-mayo sauce mixture into the pan and stir briskly until the sauce thickens slightly and coats the pork, calamari and beans well. Be careful not to let the mixture simmer and cook too long as the pork will become overcooked and dry and the calamari rubbery.

Transfer to a large bowl and garnish with fresh coriander. Serve immediately.

TERIYAKI CROQUETTES

We call this dish 'korokke' and it is a very traditional Japanese/Western everyday dish, like 'karei raisu', or curry rice. Basically these are potato croquettes with minced teriyaki beef, although other types of meat can be used if you like.

MAKES 8-10

4 medium-sized potatoes, peeled and quartered
1 teaspoon sunflower oil
½ large onion, chopped
150g minced beef, pork or chicken thigh
¼ teaspoon salt
¼ teaspoon ground white pepper
2 tablespoons soy sauce
1 tablespoon mirin
1 tablespoon sugar
1 large egg
4 tablespoons plain flour
75g panko breadcrumbs
1 litre oil, for deep-frying
tonkatsu sauce (page 84) or Worcestershire sauce, to serve
crisp salad leaves, to serve

Boil the potatoes with plenty of water in a large pan with a pinch of salt for 10–12 minutes until just cooked. Be very careful not to overboil the potatoes otherwise your croquettes will become too wet.

Meanwhile, heat a frying pan, add the sunflower oil and fry the onion for 2 minutes, add the mince and then season with the salt and pepper. Continue to fry for a further 2 minutes over medium heat, then reduce the heat to low and add the soy sauce, mirin and sugar. Cook for a further 2–3 minutes, or until most of the liquid has evaporated. Leave it to cool down slightly in the pan.

Once the potatoes are cooked, drain and leave them in a colander to steam-dry for 1 minute, put the potatoes back into the pan and cook over low heat for 1 minute (this gets rid of excess water). Mash the potatoes with a vegetable masher or fork.

Add the meat mixture, along with any juices in the pan, to the mashed potatoes and mix well using your hands. Divide the mixture into 8–10 balls and flatten into oval-shaped discs.

Beat the egg in a bowl and put the flour and breadcrumbs on separate plates. Dust each croquette with flour first, dip it into the egg then into the breadcrumbs to coat. Repeat for the remaining pieces.

Heat the oil in a frying pan over medium-high heat to reach 180°C/350°F. Carefully add the croquettes and deep-fry them for 3–4 minutes until golden brown. If necessary fry in batches. Use a slotted spoon to remove them and serve hot with tonkatsu sauce or Worcestershire sauce. Fresh and crispy salad leaves make great accompaniments.

WAFU MISO STEAK

Marinating meat or fish in miso is a very traditional Japanese cooking method. The marinating process cures the meat, enhancing and adding to its flavour.

SERVES 4

4 × 120g thin sirloin steaks
200g miso paste
150g white miso paste
4 tablespoons mirin
4 tablespoons caster sugar
1 bunch chives, finely chopped, to serve
sansho pepper, to sprinkle, optional

For the cauliflower purée
800g cauliflower
800ml soy milk
1 teaspoon instant dashi powder
1 tablespoon mirin
2 teaspoons Dijon mustard, optional
4 egg yolks
salt

Trim any excess fat from the steaks. Put both miso pastes, the mirin and the sugar in a bowl and mix well until smooth.

In a shallow square dish, smear half of the miso mixture on the bottom surface to cover it. Lay the steaks on top in a single layer, making sure to leave a bit of a gap between each one. Pour over the remaining miso mixture and spread to coat the top of the steaks. Cover with cling film and allow to marinate for at least 12–24 hours in the fridge.

Cut the cauliflower into large bite-sized chunks and put in a saucepan with the soy milk and ½ teaspoon salt. Bring to the boil, cover with the lid and simmer for 5–6 minutes or until the cauliflower is soft enough for a toothpick to poke through easily. Drain and reserve 150ml of the cooking liquid.

Immediately transfer the cauliflower to a food processor with a pinch of salt, the kombu dashi powder, mirin and mustard if you like. Blitz until it becomes a purée (you can also use a stick blender). If it feels too stiff, add some of the reserved cauliflower soy milk, checking the texture as you go. Add the egg yolks and blitz slowly, taking care it doesn't become too airy. Cover and keep warm.

Take the steak out of the fridge at least 1 hour before cooking. Preheat the grill to high. Remove the steak from the marinade, wiping any excess off with kitchen paper. Lay the steaks on the grill rack and grill for about 2 minutes on each side taking care not to burn them. Leave the steaks to rest for 5 minutes, then slice up.

To serve, spread some of the cauliflower purée on a plate, lay beef slices on top and sprinkle with a generous amount of chopped chives. Serve with the sansho pepper sprinkled on top, if you wish.

BEEF CUBES WITH JAPANESE TOMATO SAUCE

Tomato is one of the most popular vegetables in Japan; it can be used for traditional Japanese, fusion or Western dishes. Here the tomato shows its versatility in my Japanese version of tomato sauce with simple rare steak.

SERVES 4

250ml sunflower or corn oil
1 garlic bulb, cloves peeled and thinly sliced
4 × 150g beef fillets
1 teaspoon salt
1 teaspoon pepper

For the Japanese tomato sauce
240ml tomato juice
120ml soy sauce
4 tablespoons mirin
1 onion, finely chopped
50g grated carrot
1 garlic clove, finely chopped
1½ tablespoons finely grated ginger
60–80g clear honey

First, make the tomato sauce. Put all the ingredients except for the honey in a saucepan and bring to a simmer. Cook gently for about 10 minutes, or until the liquid has reduced by about 20 per cent, then turn off the heat. Add about half of the honey first, and taste. If you prefer it sweeter, add more honey. This sauce can be made in advance as it will keep well in the fridge for 1 week.

Heat the oil in a small saucepan over very low heat. Fry the sliced garlic in the warm oil very slowly – you should see tiny little bubbles around the garlic but no sizzling. Maintain this temperature and cook the garlic for about 10 minutes; the garlic should still be white at this stage. Turn up the heat slightly and as soon as the garlic starts to turn slightly golden, remove with a slotted spoon, transfer onto layered kitchen paper and set aside.

To cook the steak, trim off any sinew from the fillets. Cut the beef into bite-sized cubes and season with salt and pepper. Heat a large frying pan over medium-high heat, add the steak cubes making sure that the cubes are not touching (you may need to do this in batches). Cook for 1 minute, turn the heat to medium, and then turn over to cook the other side. Try to cook all sides of each cube of beef for about 40 seconds–1 minute per side (although the exact timing will depend on how well done you prefer the steak).

Take the beef out of the pan, cover loosely with foil and leave to rest for a few minutes.

While the beef is resting, quickly heat up the sauce. Dollop some sauce into the centre of each serving plate or wide bowl, place the seared beef cubes on top of the sauce and lastly top with a generous amount of the crispy garlic.

VEAL FILLET WITH GINGER, SOY AND BLUE CHEESE SAUCE

Ginger and blue cheese? You'll either love or hate this. The sharpness of the ginger cuts through the richness of the cheese, and the silky sauce they make combines well with subtle meats like veal and pork fillet.

SERVES 4

30g miso paste

2 tablespoons mirin

4 tablespoons vegetable oil, plus extra for brushing and frying

4 veal (or pork) fillets, approx. 800g

200g cauliflower

300g spinach leaves

fine salad leaves (watercress, rocket, lamb's lettuce), to serve, optional

1 tablespoon mixed toasted black and white sesame seeds, to serve

salt and ground white pepper

For the ginger, soy and blue cheese sauce

320ml dashi stock (page 28)

2 tablespoons soy sauce

60ml mirin

2 tablespoons sake

60g blue cheese

40g grated ginger

1 teaspoon cornflour

Mix the miso paste, mirin and vegetable oil in a bowl, then rub this mixture all over the veal fillets. Cut the cauliflower into about 3cm-thick slices, keeping the floret shape.

Preheat the oven to 180°C/350°F/Gas Mark 4. Heat an ovenproof frying pan over medium-high heat, brush the veal lightly with vegetable oil and quickly sear all over until browned. Loosely cover with foil, transfer to the oven and cook for 6–7 minutes. Take it out of the oven, turn the veal over and cook for a further 2–3 minutes or until the veal is cooked to your preference. Cooking time varies depending on the thickness of veal and how rare you like it. Remove and let the veal rest for 5–6 minutes.

If using pork fillets, make sure to remove the sinew and cut into about 2.5cm thick steaks. Cook as per the veal above.

While the veal is cooking, make the sauce. Heat the stock, soy sauce, mirin and sake in a small saucepan, stirring well. Once the sauce comes to the boil, crumble the blue cheese into the pan, and continue to stir until the cheese melts and the sauce thickens. Add the grated ginger and simmer for a further 1 minute. Remove from the heat and strain the sauce through a fine sieve. Taste and adjust the seasoning to taste – if the sauce is too salty, add a little more mirin. Turn off the heat for now.

Heat some oil in a frying pan and fry both sides of cauliflower for 2 minutes on each side. Season with salt and pepper. Take the cauliflower out and set aside, then quickly stir-fry the spinach for 20 seconds and season with a pinch of salt and pepper. Remove the spinach to drain on a kitchen paper, then lightly squeeze to remove excess moisture.

Put the sauce back on the heat and bring to the boil. In a small bowl, mix the cornflour with 1 tablespoon water until smooth and pour this into the pan, stirring all the time until thickened to the consistency of double cream. Turn off the heat.

Cut the veal into slices about 7mm thick and place on top of the spinach on each plate. Pour the sauce over the veal and then place the fried cauliflower on the side. Sprinkle with a few fine salad leaves, if using, and the sesame seeds.

GRILLED DUCK WITH PLUM MISO ON MAGNOLIA LEAVES

The sourness of the plum and richness of the *hatcho* miso is a perfect match with duck. The scent of magnolia leaves blends in with the whole dish beautifully.

SERVES 2

2 large duck breast fillets

4 fresh magnolia leaves

pinch of salt

pinch of sansho pepper

4 spring onions

120g hatcho miso and/or red miso paste

2–3 ripe plums, destoned and diced

4 shiitake mushrooms, finely chopped

125ml sake

60ml mirin

2 tablespoons soft brown sugar

2 teaspoons toasted white sesame seeds, to sprinkle

Trim and remove any sinew from the duck breasts and score the skin, ensuring not to cut through into the flesh.

Preheat the oven to 120°C/230°F/Gas Mark 1. Place the magnolia leaves on a tray in the oven to dry for a 3–4 minutes, being careful not to let them burn. Set aside.

Heat a dry frying pan over medium-high heat, add the duck breasts, skin-side down, and season with the salt and sansho pepper. Sear for 1 minute to let the fat render, then turn over and cook for another minute until browned. Increase the heat and turn the duck again to sear, skin-side down, for 2 minutes. Remove from the heat and set the duck aside.

Finely chop the spring onions, keeping a small amount of the green part for the garnish.

Mix the red miso with 125ml water in a small saucepan and bring to a simmer slowly, stirring to ensure the paste is loose. Add the chopped spring onions, plums, mushrooms, sake, mirin and sugar, and stir. Bring to the boil over medium heat, reduce to low heat and simmer for 5–6 minutes or until the mixture becomes a thick paste.

Preheat the grill to medium-high heat. Slice the duck thinly and use the back of a spoon to spread a thin layer of the miso mixture onto each magnolia leaf. Place the duck breast slices on top and then cover the meat with the remaining miso. Lay on an oven tray and grill the duck for 4 minutes, until the miso begins to bubble, and remove before it starts to burn.

Finely chop the reserved green part of the spring onions and sprinkle over the duck along with the sesame seeds. Serve immediately.

GUINEAFOWL WITH MISO SWEETCORN PURÉE

Two authentic Japanese ingredients go well with butter: one is soy sauce and the other is miso, which I use here. I also like to grill sweet corncobs with soy sauce and butter, and I remember my father used to eat rice with a little miso and butter.

SERVES 4

2 lemons
2 whole guineafowls
2 tablespoons vegetable or sunflower oil
4 large heads of pak choi
2 tablespoons roasted sesame oil
2 tablespoons toasted sesame seeds, ground
salt and freshly ground black pepper

For the miso sweetcorn purée
2 large sweet corncobs or 100g tinned sweetcorn, drained
40g slightly salted butter
4 tablespoons miso paste

Preheat the oven to 180°C/350°F/Gas Mark 4. Cut the lemons in half and stuff into the guineafowls.

Heat the oil in a large frying pan and lightly season the guineafowls with salt and pepper. Sear all surfaces of the birds until light golden in colour all over.

Transfer the birds to a baking tray, cover with foil and roast in the oven for about 30 minutes. Take off the foil, then continue to cook for another 20–30 minutes, taking care not to overcook them.

Melt 20g butter and brush the corncobs with it, then put them in a roasting tin. Bake in the oven for about 30 minutes at the same time as the guineafowls, turning them a few times. Take both of them out of the oven and rest the guinea fowl for 10 minutes, loosely covered.

When the corn is cool enough to handle, cut off the kernels and put them in a food processor (if using tinned sweetcorn, add these now). Blitz to make a very smooth purée. Add the miso paste, 2 tablespoons water and remaining 20g butter and blitz again. If the consistency is too stiff, add a little more water to loosen. Season to taste with salt and pepper.

Next, cut the pak choi into quarters vertically (if the heads are small, cut them in half) and wash well between the stems. Steam for 3–4 minutes, or until the stems are just cooked through and still have bite.

To carve the guineafowl, use a sharp knife to first cut the wings and legs off. Next, carefully fillet the breasts by sliding the filleting knife along the bones, taking care and trying not to leave too much meat on the bones.

To assemble, arrange the guineafowl meat on serving plates with the miso sweetcorn purée, then add the pak choi. Drizzle a little sesame oil and sprinkle toasted and ground sesame seeds over the dish and serve.

CHICKEN IN HOT AND SOUR BROTH

An incredibly easy and quick dish that makes use of ordinary storecupboard and fridge ingredients yet is still very elegant. Try to use organic chicken and kombu sprinkles as both will lend a deeper flavour to the dish.

SERVES 4

4 large boneless chicken thighs,
   preferably organic, with skin on
2 teaspoons salt
500ml sake
500ml rice vinegar
200ml soy sauce
200ml mirin
1 teaspoon sugar
½ teaspoon kombu sprinkles, optional
4–6 large extra mild green chillies,
   finely sliced
1 bunch of spring onions, white part
   only
2–3 teaspoons mustard, optional

Trim off any excess fat from the chicken thighs and sprinkle with a little salt. Leave them for about 15 minutes.

Heat a frying pan over medium heat and fry the chicken, skin-side down, for a couple of minutes or until they have slightly caramelised. Turn them over and fry the other side for about 1 minute. Remove from the heat and pour around 150ml boiling water over the chicken to rinse off the salt and fat, then pat dry with kitchen paper.

Put 500ml water, the sake, rice vinegar, soy sauce, mirin, sugar and, if using, kombu sprinkles in a large saucepan and bring to the boil over high heat. Add the chicken to the pan and reduce the heat to medium-low. Simmer for 7–8 minutes.

While the chicken is simmering, fry the green chillies over medium heat in the same frying pan used to brown the chicken. This will only take a few minutes. Then add the fried chillies to the pan with the chicken.

Continue to cook the chicken and green chillies for a further 3–4 minutes.

Slice the spring onions very thinly and on the diagonal, place in a bowl of ice-cold water and soak.

Take the chicken out of the broth using tongs, and slice into bite-sized pieces. Place in a wide bowl. (If you have a blowtorch, you can quickly char the skin of the chicken before slicing). Ladle the broth over the chicken into the bowl, and then place a few green chilli pieces alongside the chicken.

Drain the spring onions and pat them dry with kitchen paper. Scatter on the top of the chicken, then dot with a little mustard if you like.

CHICKEN AND VEGETABLE KATSU

Tonkatsu is a well-known and popular dish amongst Japanese and Western people. However, it is quite rich and at its heart is just deep-fried crumbed pork. As much as I love tonkatsu, I hesitate… So I have created this chicken and vegetable katsu, a much lighter and less calorific version of its original.

SERVES 4

400g boneless and skinless chicken breasts, about 2

1 carrot, very thinly sliced using a mandoline

1 courgette, very thinly sliced using a mandoline

2 eggs

2 teaspoons Dijon mustard

130g buckwheat flour

150g panko breadcrumbs

1.5 litres vegetable or sunflower oil, for deep-frying

salt and freshly ground black pepper

To serve

thinly sliced cabbage or crisp salad leaves

1 lemon, cut into wedges

tonkatsu sauce (page 84)

Slice each chicken breast on a slant, lengthways, into 4 pieces and then pound each slice with a meat tenderiser (or rolling pin). Pound repeatedly to make even, thin chicken pieces about the thickness of sandwich bread.

Bring a saucepan of water to the boil with a pinch of salt and then add the carrot slices followed by the courgette slices. Cook for 1 minute over high heat, drain and leave in a colander to steam-dry.

Lay a chicken slice on a chopping board and season with salt and pepper. Next, put a few carrot and courgette slices on top of the chicken. Lastly, place another chicken slice on top to sandwich the vegetables together, and then sprinkle over a little salt and pepper. Secure the edges closed with toothpicks. Repeat this process with the remaining chicken slices to make a total of 4 'sandwiches'.

In a small bowl, beat the eggs with the mustard. Scatter the flour on a plate and do the same with the breadcrumbs.

Dredge the entire chicken and vegetable sandwich with flour, dip it into the egg mixture, then into the breadcrumbs making sure that all of the chicken is completely covered with crumbs (press them down lightly to ensure they stick). Repeat for the remaining pieces.

Heat the oil in a deep frying pan or wok to 160°C/320°F. Carefully place the chicken into the hot oil and deep-fry for about 2 minutes. Turn over and cook for a further 2 minutes, or until lightly golden in colour. Use a slotted spoon to remove the chicken from the oil and drain on kitchen paper. When cool enough to handle, carefully remove the cocktail sticks.

Serve the katsu with very thinly sliced and crispy fresh cabbage or salad leaves and lemon wedges and tonkatsu sauce on the side.

CHICKEN BREAST WITH YAKUMI SAUCE

This is my number one dish from this book. It's absolutely delicious, extremely healthy and low in calories. Make lots of *yakumi* sauce and use leftovers to serve with any grilled or steamed white meat or fish.

SERVES 4

600g boneless chicken breasts, with
    skin on
2 teaspoons salt
2 teaspoons sugar
1 leek, roughly chopped
20g ginger, sliced
2 tablespoons sake
1 teaspoon ground white pepper
1 pointed cabbage, trimmed and cut
    into 8 individual pieces
handful of coriander leaves, chopped
sesame seeds, to sprinkle, optional
salt and freshly ground black pepper

For the yakumi sauce
4 tablespoons soy sauce
2 tablespoons rice vinegar
2 tablespoons sesame oil
1½ tablespoons grated ginger
2 tablespoons oyster sauce
1½ tablespoons miso paste
2 tablespoons sugar
1 red chilli, finely chopped
4 tablespoons finely chopped spring
    onion
4 tablespoons finely chopped
    coriander

Take the skin off the chicken breasts and sprinkle with 1 teaspoon mixed salt and pepper. Leave to sit for 10 minutes.

To make the crispy chicken skin, preheat the oven to 220°C/430°F/Gas Mark 7. Place the chicken skin on a baking sheet lined with baking parchment and lightly season with salt. Place another layer of parchment on top of the skin and weigh it down using an oven tray (to keep the skin flat). Bake for 10–15 minutes, or until crisp, keeping an eye on it to ensure it doesn't burn. Remove and set aside to cool.

Fill a large pan with 1 litre water, add the salt, sugar, leek, ginger, sake, white pepper and the chicken breasts. Bring to the boil, turn the heat down to medium-low and cook with a lid on for 10 minutes taking care not to let it boil.

Take off the lid, put the cabbage pieces on top of the chicken, cover with the lid and cook for a further 8–10 minutes. Turn the heat off and, using tongs, take the cabbage out of the broth and drain in a colander. Leave the chicken to steep in the broth for 20–30 minutes – this way the chicken stays moist and becomes more flavoursome.

Meanwhile, make the yakumi sauce by stirring together the ingredients. This can be made up to 1 week in advance and stored in the fridge.

To serve, remove the chicken breasts from the pan and onto a chopping board. Pat dry the cabbage leaves and arrange them on the plate. Cut the chicken breast into 1cm-thick slices and place them on top of the cabbage leaves.

Pour the yakumi sauce over the chicken (or serve on the side) and sprinkle with sesame seeds and chopped coriander leaves. Break the chicken skin in half and place on top of the chicken.

Note: You can also serve the chicken cold. Just heat up the broth, season with a dash of soy sauce and add some chopped spring onions. Serve the broth as a soup on the side.

VEGETABLES AND SEAWEED

Whether in soups, stews, fish dishes or served with tofu, Japan's great variety of vegetables make up much of our food. Pickled vegetables, called *tsukemono*, accompany most meals, and there are several different pickling methods, the oldest being *nukazuke*, a complicated process which my mother was adept at. I remember watching her take a bowl of wet *nuka* (made from rice bran mixed with sugar and salt) and digging a little hole in which she would bury whole cucumbers and eggplants. They would only take one or two days to pickle and would be embued with a deep vegetable flavour and a sweet and sour kick. To this day, I need to have *tsukemono* with my rice. Pickling can be time-consuming, taking weeks to preserve in some cases, but pickles are a must for almost all Japanese meals – their sour taste and crunchy texture accents spice and sweetness. I like to make a quicker version by mixing dashi stock with vinegar, seaweed and perhaps a dash of chilli or fresh ginger. Once the desired vegetable has been rubbed all over with this mix, along with salt, and then chopped into small pieces, it only needs to be left for half a day to marinate.

As I grew up in Kyoto, I was lucky enough to enjoy the seasonal and unique products that grow on the surrounding mountainsides, such as *takenoko* (bamboo shoots). My mother used to make a delicious dish of *takenoko* and *wakame* seaweed; the combination of crunchy bamboo shoots and the melt-in-the-mouth seaweed is simple, everyday, but divine. What is not quite so simple is the bamboo shoot preparation, which involves peeling away the thick outer husks, slicing off the tip and boiling until soft enough to remove the inner sheaths. My mother would scurry around quietly in the kitchen, working away until she was left with something that might look a bit like a miniature rhinoceros's horn – pointed, cream and ringed from base to tip.

The mountains are also a haven for mushrooms, which are known as the only vegan and non-fortified dietary source of vitamin D – a vitamin which those of us that work inside can be lacking in. Not only extremely good for you, Japanese mushrooms also add a unique umami flavour to any dish, and I'm thrilled that they're now so easy to find in UK supermarkets.

Another Japanese ingredient which is now becoming popular all over the world is seaweed, although this fantastic ingredient has been eaten in Japan for over 10,000 years. A 'superfood', it has a wide range of unique health benefits: it is blood purifying, high in iron, vitamin C and iodine, detoxifying and contains ten times more calcium than an equivalent portion of milk. Seaweed has antioxidant properties that are also much higher and more complex than many other vegetables, and it even contains minerals with anti-inflammatory, anticoagulant, antithrombotic, anticancer and antiviral benefits – it is even believed to have antibiotic properties effective against penicillin-resistant bacteria.

There are many different types of seaweed although my personal favourite is *kombu*, which is used to flavour dashi stock and soups, although I also use it to add a smoky saltiness to Western dishes like tomato sauce. Other common varieties include *nori,* which is used in its dried form to wrap sushi; *wakame*, which has a delicate flavour and is perfect in light salads; and *dulse*, a dark red seaweed with purifying properties. Two of the most miraculous seaweeds are *arame* – which is sweet and mild, known to be the ocean's richest source of iodine and phytohormones, and therefore a remedy for health problems such as fibroids, adhesions and menopausal symptoms – and black *hijiki* seaweed – which has the most calcium of any sea vegetable.

Seaweed is also believed to prevent wrinkles, and to promote soft skin and strong, glossy hair. This is perhaps one of the reasons for the youthful appearance of many Japanese men and women.

VEGETARIAN GYOZA DUMPLINGS

These dumplings are a staple in my kitchen. They are my tried and tested vegetarian gyoza with a satisfying filling packed with flavour. Tofu and mushroom are not the only meat substitute for a vegetarian dumpling!

SERVES 4

50–60 gyoza dumpling wrappers
3 tablespoons vegetable or sunflower
   oil
1–2 tablespoons chilli paste, to serve

For the filling
20g dried shiitake mushrooms
80g tinned chickpeas, drained
2 tablespoons sesame oil
80g tinned sweetcorn, drained
50g tinned water chestnuts, drained
½ small pointed cabbage, finely
   chopped
1 bunch of spring onions, finely
   chopped
1 bunch of coriander, finely chopped
1 tablespoon grated ginger
1 tablespoon soy sauce
¼ teaspoon ground white pepper
2 teaspoons mirin
1 teaspoon sake
1–2 teaspoons cornflour, as needed

For the dipping sauce
3 tablespoons soy sauce
2 tablespoons rice vinegar
2 tablespoons mirin
1 tablespoon roasted sesame oil
2 tablespoons toasted and ground
   white sesame seeds

First prepare the filling. Soak the dried shiitake mushrooms in a bowl of water for 1 hour. Drain, squeeze out excess water and finely chop the shiitake mushrooms.

Put the chickpeas in a food processor or blender with the sesame oil and blitz to form a smooth texture. Chop the sweetcorn roughly and put in a large bowl along with the puréed chickpeas. Add the remaining filling ingredients and mix well using your hands – the consistency should be firm enough to form a ball but not too dry. If you feel the filling is too wet, then add a little more cornflour.

Place a wrapper in the palm of your left hand and dab two-thirds of the edges with water. Place a teaspoonful of the filling in the centre of the wrapper and fold over, making small pinched creases to seal the edges together. Repeat for the rest of the filling until you run out of wrappers or filling.

Heat 2 tablespoons oil in a large pan over medium-high heat, and then carefully add the dumplings in lines. Pour 120ml water into the pan and partially cover with a lid, making sure there is a decent gap between the lip of the pan and the lid, so that some steam can escape. Cook over medium heat for 5 minutes or until all of the water has evaporated.

Take the lid off and turn up the heat to high, add the remaining 1 tablespoon oil to the pan, then cook for a further 1 minute or until the base of the dumplings are brown and crisp.

Meanwhile, combine the dipping sauce ingredients in a small bowl.

To serve, use a palette knife to scoop up a line of dumplings and quickly turn over onto the plate, crispy side up. Serve immediately with the dipping sauce and chilli paste on the side.

VEGETABLES AND SEAWEED 139

ASPARAGUS AND UMAMI DASHI JELLY WITH ONSEN TAMAGO

There is nothing as satisfying as a perfectly cooked runny egg yolk. Traditionally prepared in hot spring water, *onsen tamago* is a slow-cooked egg that has been poached to just the right level inside its shell. The whites are soft and silky and the yolks are creamy, making them simply ideal for asparagus dipping. This dish could be thought of as a Japanese version of the classic asparagus with hollandaise sauce.

SERVES 4

4 large eggs, at room temperature
   (around 10–15°C)
12 large asparagus spears
1 teaspoon salt
1 teaspoon black sesame seeds

For the umami dashi jelly
360ml dashi stock (page 28)
3 tablespoons sake
3 tablespoons mirin
3 tablespoons soy sauce
17g agar-agar flakes

First, make the umami dashi jelly. Whisk the ingredients in a saucepan until the agar-agar is completely dissolved. Place the pan over medium heat and warm until it reaches 70°C/160°F, making sure it doesn't reach boiling point. Turn off the heat once it gets to temperature and then put the base of the pan into a sink filled with cold water. Whisk all the time as the mixture cools. Put in the fridge to set to a wobbly jelly. (You can keep this mixture in the fridge for about 1 week, but if using gelatine note that the jelly will be slightly firmer.)

Make the *onsen tamago* next. Fill a heavy-based saucepan with water, cover and bring to the boil. Turn the heat off and then add 200ml water. Gently slide the eggs into the warm water and put the lid back on. Leave the eggs to soak for about 18 minutes. The soaking time may vary slightly depending on the room temperature, size of the egg, thickness of the pan… It is a chemistry to perfect *onsen tamago*!

Prepare the asparagus by trimming the hard base from the spears. In a large saucepan bring plenty of water to the boil with the salt. Add the asparagus to the pan, boil for 3 minutes over high heat, or until just tender. Rinse immediately with cold water, which helps retain the bright green colour of the asparagus. Drain and pat dry with kitchen paper.

To serve, place 3 large asparagus spears diagonally on each plate and then crack an egg on top. Slice the umami dashi jelly and place atop the egg. Finish with a little scattering of black sesame seeds.

BUTTERNUT SQUASH WITH OKRA AND ALMOND

This dish is a slight twist from traditional Japanese pumpkin dishes in its use of okra and almond flakes. Roasting the butternut squash intensifies its flavour, adding okra provides freshness, and the almonds add a lovely texture.

SERVES 4

1 butternut squash or kabocha
   pumpkin
4 tablespoons sunflower oil and/or
   pumpkin seed oil
½ teaspoon sea salt
4 tablespoons flaked almonds
750ml dashi stock (page 28) or 1½
   teaspoons instant dashi powder
3 tablespoons mirin
3 tablespoons soy sauce
30g ginger, thinly sliced
1 teaspoon kombu sprinkles
200g okra
1 teaspoon cornflour mixed with 2
   tablespoons water

Preheat the oven to 180°C/350°F/Gas Mark 4. Cut the butternut squash in half, then slice the skin off. Using a spoon, scrape out the seeds and roughly cut the squash into 3–4cm chunks.

In an oven tray, toss the squash chunks in the oil and sea salt and then roast for about 15 minutes. Turn the pieces around so they don't burn on one side and return the tray to the oven to roast the squash for a further 10 minutes. Scatter the flaked almonds over a small baking tray and toast in the oven for 5 minutes.

Remove both the squash and almonds from the oven. Tip the squash into a large serving bowl and set aside with the almonds.

While the squash is roasting, heat the dashi stock in a saucepan. Once it comes to the boil, add the mirin, soy sauce, ginger and kombu sprinkles and simmer for a few minutes.

Cut the okra in half diagonally. Bring the stock back to the boil, add the okra and cook for 2–3 minutes. Add the cornflour mixture, stirring all the time until thickened.

Ladle the soup over the butternut squash in the bowl, then sprinkle the almonds over the whole dish and serve.

MOCHI AND RAINBOW VEG WITH KOMBU BUTTER SAUCE

Here is a fun combination of flavours and textures in one dish. The small amount of butter pairs beautifully with soy sauce and kombu adding a richness. Mochi gives this dish an extra dimension, being like a sticky rice cake.

SERVES 4

300g kabocha pumpkin or butternut
    squash
1 litre vegetarian stock (page 28)
2 tablespoons soy sauce
2 tablespoons mirin
pinch of salt
8 baby courgettes
8–12 baby corn
1 red pepper
1 tablespoon vegetable oil
4 squares mochi (Japanese rice cake)
    (around 200g)
5cm piece ginger, finely sliced, to
    garnish
salt and freshly ground black pepper

For the kombu butter sauce
2 teaspoons kombu sprinkles
40g butter
½ onion, finely chopped
100g broccoli, finely chopped

First, prepare the pumpkin by cutting it into large bite-sized chunks. If you have a microwave, cut the pumpkin into quarters, wrap in cling film, then microwave on medium for 2 minutes – this way the pumpkin will soften slightly making it easier to cut. Using a sharp knife, scrape off the sharp edges of each pumpkin chunk so you have rounded edges – this way, each chunk will hold its shape when cooked. This smoothing down of angles is called 'mentori'.

Heat the vegetarian stock, soy sauce, mirin and salt in a saucepan and add the pumpkin. Cook, covered and undisturbed, for about 5 minutes, or until the pumpkin becomes soft. Remove the pumpkin from the stock and set both to one side.

Preheat the grill to medium-high. Cut the courgettes and baby corn in half vertically. Remove the seeds from the pepper and cut into quarters. Place the courgettes, baby corn and pepper on a grill rack and brush the oil all over. Grill the vegetables for 4 minutes, then turn over and grill for a further 3 minutes or until almost cooked. Next, add the mochi squares to the grill and cook for about 2 minutes on each side. Take the vegetables and mochi out of the grill.

While the vegetables and mochi are grilling, reheat the stock used for cooking the pumpkin. Add 30g butter, the kombu sprinkles, finely chopped onion and broccoli, and simmer for 5 minutes, until the onion and broccoli are meltingly soft.

Transfer the contents of the pan to a blender or food processor and blitz to a thick sauce. Return to the pan and bring to the boil. Check the seasoning once it comes to a boil, turn off the heat and stir in the remaining 10g butter.

Assemble all the vegetables and mochi nicely within individual shallow bowls and pour the kombu butter sauce around the vegetables so as not to cover all the components. Garnish with the thinly sliced ginger.

CLOUDY SOUP

This is such a comforting soup, and so quick to cook. Daikon radish is crucial here for both flavour and texture. In Japanese, this soup is call 'Mizore' meaning 'sleet'.

SERVES 4

1 sheet deep-fried tofu
1 litre dashi stock (page 28) or 2
   teaspoons instant dashi powder
   mixed with water
½ medium carrot, cut into fine
   matchsticks
2 tablespoons sake
2 tablespoons mirin
½ teaspoon salt, plus extra to season
3 tablespoons soy sauce
1 tablespoon cornflour mixed with 1
   tablespoon water
200g daikon radish, peeled and finely
   grated
2 tablespoons finely chopped spring
   onions
seven-spice powder, to serve

Bring a saucepan of water to the boil and blanch the deep-fried tofu for a few minutes. Drain, allow to cool enough to handle, then squeeze out the excess water. Slice the tofu sheet into 5 × 40mm pieces.

Put the dashi stock in a saucepan, bring to the boil and add the tofu, carrot, sake, mirin and salt, then simmer over medium-low heat for about 2 minutes. Add the soy sauce, turn up the heat to high, pour in the cornflour mixture and let it simmer for about 1 minute, stirring at all times, until the broth has slightly thickened.

Keeping the pan over high heat, add the grated daikon and taste to adjust the seasoning with salt, soy sauce or mirin.

Pour the soup into individual bowls and sprinkle over the finely chopped spring onions. Serve immediately with the seven-spice powder on the side.

UMAMI TOMATO SOUP WITH TOFU CROUTONS

Minimalism can be stunning. Fusion can be tasty. This dish is a great example of the two. And when I eat this dish, it makes me feel clean yet surreal.

SERVES 4

1 tablespoon olive oil

25g butter

1 large onion, finely chopped

1kg large ripe tomatoes, peeled and chopped or 3 × 400g tinned tomatoes

125ml white wine or sake

2 teaspoons instant dashi powder

1 tablespoon balsamic vinegar

½ teaspoon dried chilli flakes, or to taste

fresh green herbs, such as mint, basil or coriander, to garnish

salt and freshly ground black pepper

For the tofu croutons

200g firm tofu

2 tablespoons vegetable, corn or sunflower oil

2 tablespoons cornflour

1 tablespoon instant dashi powder

First, cut the tofu into 2cm cubes and wrap them in kitchen paper. Set aside.

Heat the olive oil in a large saucepan over medium heat and add the butter. Add the finely chopped onion to the pan and sauté for about 10 minutes until transparent and softened.

Add the peeled tomatoes or tinned tomatoes to the pan together with the white wine or sake and then season with a pinch of salt and pepper. Bring to the boil and then add the dashi powder, balsamic vinegar and chilli flakes. Stir well, turn the heat down slightly and simmer, covered, for 15–20 minutes.

Meanwhile, make the tofu croutons. Heat the oil in a frying pan or wok over medium heat. Season the cornflour with the dashi powder, salt and pepper and use this to dust the drained tofu cubes. Stir-fry the tofu cubes over medium-low heat until the surface appears crisp but not browned. Remove from the pan with a slotted spoon and transfer to kitchen paper to drain.

To serve, pour the tomato soup into individual bowls and place a pile of the tofu croutons in the centre. Garnish with your choice of fresh green herbs.

PICKLED COURGETTE AND SAMPHIRE

In the Japanese diet, pickled vegetables, miso soup and rice go hand in hand. I enjoy eating lightly pickled vegetables as a side salad as they add a colourful, clean and fresh dimension to any given meal.

SERVES 4

200g samphire

2 courgettes

1 teaspoon salt

40g ginger, peeled and sliced into very fine matchsticks

1 red chilli, thinly sliced

80g pickled ginger, drained and roughly chopped

1 tablespoon toasted sesame seeds

For the pickling liquid

350ml rice vinegar

1 teaspoon instant dashi powder

2 teaspoons kombu sprinkles

1½ tablespoons sugar

Mix all the ingredients for the pickling liquid with 100ml water in a small saucepan and then bring to a simmer for 2 minutes. Turn off the heat and let the liquid cool.

Bring a saucepan of water to the boil and blanch the samphire for 1 minute, then drain under cold running water until cooled.

Cut each courgette into 4 chunks first, then cut each chunk into 2 vertically. Slice each chunk into 2mm thick pieces so they are fat strips. Put the sliced courgettes into a colander, sprinkle over the salt and gently rub the salt into the courgettes. Lightly rinse under cold running water and drain.

Mix the courgettes, samphire, ginger and chilli in a bowl and then pour in the pickling liquid. Stir well, put a similar sized bowl on top and place a heavy jar or tin inside to weigh it down. Keep the whole assembly in the fridge for at least 1 hour and up to 3 hours.

Just before serving, drain about 70 per cent of the pickling liquid (you may reserve the pickling liquid and use it for other vegetables) and quickly mix the pickled ginger and toasted sesame seeds with the vegetables.

Note: This dish is best consumed immediately as the samphire will discolour if you leave it too long beyond the 3 hours above.

SESAME LOTUS ROOT SALAD

Kinpira, as it's known in Japan, is a classic dish that traditionally uses burdock root and is still popular today. In this dish, *renkon* (lotus root) is used to provide quite an addictive crunch.

SERVES 4

200g lotus root
1 tablespoon rice vinegar
1 teaspoon salt, plus extra to season
100g mangetout (or sugar snap peas)
1 large carrot
2 tablespoons vegetable oil
2 red chillies, thinly sliced
2 tablespoons soy sauce
1½ tablespoons mirin
2 teaspoons sugar
1 teaspoon roasted sesame oil
1 tablespoon toasted white sesame seeds

Peel the lotus root and cut thinly into 5mm thick slices. If the lotus root is fat, cut the whole root into two horizontally first, then slice to make bite-sized pieces.

In a bowl, mix the vinegar with 750ml water and add the sliced lotus root. Allow to soak for at least 30 minutes. This will make the lotus root very crunchy, giving a subtle acidity to the dish.

Bring a saucepan of water and 1 teaspoon salt to the boil and blanch the mangetout for about 30 seconds. Drain and rinse under cold running water until cooled. Leave to drain in a colander and then pat dry with kitchen paper.

Peel and slice the carrot horizontally half way, then cut on the diagonal into 3mm-thick slices.

Drain the lotus root well and roughly pat dry with kitchen paper. Heat the oil in a large wok or frying pan over medium heat. Add the lotus root and stir-fry for about 2 minutes, then add the carrot and chilli along with a pinch of salt to season. Continue to stir-fry for a further 2 minutes, until the vegetables are tender.

Add the soy sauce, mirin and sugar and then cook for a further 2 minutes. Drizzle in the sesame oil, sprinkle with sesame seeds and cook for a further 30 seconds to coat the vegetables or until most of the liquid has evaporated. Stir in the mangetout, toss quickly for a final time, then turn the heat off. Serve immediately or at room temperature.

BAKED AUBERGINE WITH MISO, CHICKEN AND MOZZARELLA

This dish is based on the popular *nasu dengaku* (miso-glazed aubergine). Because miso and aubergine go together so well, I came up with this more substantial version with chicken and mozzarella that can be served as a main meal.

SERVES 4

5 tablespoons vegetable oil
160g roughly minced chicken breast
2 aubergines
160g mozzarella cheese, cubed
1 tablespoon toasted sesame seeds
salt and freshly ground black pepper

For the miso sauce and topping
40g red miso paste
40g koji miso paste
4 tablespoons mirin
1–1½ tablespoons sugar
2 tablespoons sake
1 tablespoon mayonnaise
1 teaspoon chilli paste, optional

Heat 1 tablespoon vegetable oil in a frying pan over medium heat, add the minced chicken and lightly season with salt and pepper. Fry for about 2 minutes or until the chicken just turns white and is almost cooked through.

Preheat the oven to 250°C/480°F/Gas Mark 9.

Combine all the ingredients for the miso sauce except for mayonnaise and chilli paste in a small saucepan with 125ml water. Bring to a simmer for 2–3 minutes, stirring well until all ingredients are well combined and the sauce takes on a smooth texture. Add the chicken and simmer for a further 4–5 minutes, stirring all the time, until the mixture thickens.

Cut each of the aubergines vertically into 2 with the stalk intact. Arrange the aubergine on a baking tray, cut-side up, and then brush the cut sides with the remaining oil. Bake for 16–18 minutes until very soft. If you squeeze the aubergines a little, they should be completely soft. If you feel resistance, return them to the oven and cook for a few more minutes.

Remove the aubergines from the oven and use a sharp knife to make criss-cross scores on the cut sides of the aubergines. Preheat the grill to its highest setting. While the grill heats up, stir the mayonnaise and chilli paste (if using) into the miso-chicken mixture and spread this over the scored sides of the aubergine. Top with cubes of mozzarella.

Put the aubergines back under the grill and cook under a high heat for 2–3 minutes, or until the mozzarella has just melted and the miso is bubbling – make sure the topping does not burn. Sprinkle the sesame seeds over the top and serve.

VEGETABLE TEMPURA

There is an endless menu of substantial vegetarian Japanese dishes and this is among them. Rich and meaty shiitake mushroom and crunchy baby corn is a fabulous combination. You could also try using sweetcorn if you like a bit more sweetness.

SERVES 4

120g tempura flour
125ml ice-cold water
vegetable or sunflower oil, for deep-frying
100g shiitake mushrooms, sliced
120g baby sweetcorn, cut into bite-sized pieces
100g leek, thinly sliced and layers separated

For the dipping sauce
4 tablespoons soy sauce
1 tablespoon rice vinegar
1 tablespoon lemon juice
1 teaspoon sugar
2 tablespoons very finely grated daikon radish
2 teaspoons finely grated ginger

Keep the tempura flour and water in the fridge to ensure they are very cold before cooking. If you're pressed for time, just put them in the freezer for 30 minutes. Just before cooking, mix the flour and water together to form a batter.

Mix all the dipping sauce ingredients in a bowl and set aside.

Pour enough oil in a wok or large deep frying pan to come up the sides to about 7cm and heat to 170°C/340°F. To check the temperature of the oil, drop a little batter into the pan. If the batter sinks to the bottom of the pan for more than 2 seconds, then the temperature is too low. If the batter jumps up and spits, then the temperature is too high. The batter should immediately sink to the bottom of the pan, then quickly float up to the top.

Mix the shiitake mushrooms, baby corn and leek with the cold batter in a bowl until roughly combined. The mixture should stick together but the batter should not be too thick.

Using 2 tablespoons, scoop the mixture and carefully slide it into the hot oil. (Be careful not to overcrowd the pan otherwise the tempura will become soggy.) Deep-fry the tempura for 1–2 minutes, turning over often until golden and crisp. Use a slotted spoon to remove the tempura vegetables, then drain on kitchen paper.

Serve the tempura with the dipping sauce immediately.

ARAME SEAWEED AND CALAMARI SALAD

Arame is one of my favourite seaweeds to cook with because of its ability to impart strong flavour in a short cooking time. This warm salad is a taste of the sea.

SERVES 4

40g dried arame seaweed

2 celery stalks, cut into thin
matchsticks, plus celery leaves to
garnish

½ cucumber, cut into thin matchsticks

½ onion, cut into thin matchsticks

1 tablespoon salt, plus extra to
season

½ head iceberg lettuce, shredded

200g squid, cleaned and tentacles
removed

2 tablespoons vegetable, corn or
sunflower oil

ground black pepper

For the anchovy dressing

20g anchovy fillets preserved in
oil, roughly chopped, plus 1
tablespoon anchovy oil

4 tablespoons sunflower, corn or
vegetable oil

3 tablespoons rice vinegar

½ teaspoon caster sugar

2 teaspoons soy sauce

Soak the arame seaweed in a small bowl of water for 20–30 minutes. Drain well and pat dry with kitchen paper. Cut the arame into shorter pieces if they are too long.

While the seaweed is soaking, cut all the vegetables except the lettuce, put in a colander and sprinkle over the salt. Rub all the vegetables with the salt and leave to sit for 10–15 minutes, until the moisture from them starts to come up and they become slightly softer. Rinse the vegetables well under cold running water and drain. Add the lettuce to the colander and place in the fridge with a bowl underneath to catch any remaining moisture.

Slice the squid into very thin noodles and then pat dry with kitchen paper.

Heat the oil in a frying pan until hot, then add the squid and fry over high heat for about 2 minutes, tossing as the squid cooks. Season with salt and pepper. Add the arame to the pan and stir-fry for a further 1 minute. Take the squid and arame out of the pan and drain on kitchen paper.

Pound the anchovy fillets with the remaining ingredients for the dressing using a mortar and pestle. Alternatively, do this in a small food processor or blender.

Take the vegetables out of the fridge and toss them with the squid and the dressing in a big bowl just before serving. Divide the salad between individual bowls and garnish with the leafy part of the celery if you like.

DULSE SEAWEED AND AVOCADO SALAD WITH UME DRESSING

Dulse is a new seaweed for me as we don't see much of it in Japan. It has a sea-rich flavour and stunning deep purple hue. In this recipe, I've combined it with rich and creamy avocado and tangy umeboshi (salt preserved plums), which balances nicely. It's a beautiful dish to taste and look at!

SERVES 4

50g dried dulse seaweed
100g sugar snap peas
1 onion
1 tablespoon salt
2 avocados
2 tablespoons white sesame seeds

For the ume dressing
2–3 tablespoons umeboshi (salt preserved plum) purée
4 tablespoons mirin
2 tablespoons clear honey
1 tablespoon tamari soy sauce

Soak the dulse in a bowl of cold water for 10–15 minutes and then drain and squeeze out the excess water.

Bring a saucepan of salted water to the boil and blanch the sugar snap peas for 1 minute. Drain and rinse under cold running water until the sugar snap peas become completely cool. Cut lengthways in half.

Slice the onion in half and then slice very thinly along the fibre. Place the slices in a large bowl and sprinkle over the salt, then rub vigorously into the onion until it becomes very soft and wet. Rinse very well in water to remove the salt, then squeeze out excess water.

Mix all the ingredients for the ume dressing in a large bowl until sticky and shiny.

Add the dulse and sugar snap peas to the dressing and mix well, making sure to evenly distribute the dulse. Slice the avocados in half, remove the stone and peel. Cut the flesh into segments and add to the bowl along with the onion and sesame seeds, and gently toss, taking care that the avocados don't lose their shape. Dish up the whole salad and serve.

TOFU AND EGG

To me, tofu is the most beautiful of ingredients. Very much a Japanese staple, it has been enjoyed in Japan since AD 950 and, I believe, is one of the main reasons for our population's small waistlines and silky skin. Frustratingly, tofu is a much-neglected ingredient in the West as it is often seen as a 'diet food' or a protein substitute for vegetarians. My students seem baffled when I compare tofu to cheese, but with its endless tastes, types, textures and uses, this is how I see it. In fact, in the enormous *depachika* food halls in the basements of Japanese department stores, there will be hundreds of different types of tofu – beautifully packed and from all over Japan, just like the cheese selections that you would see in France. As one of the world's healthiest foods, it is also much better for you than cheese.

Depending on the type of soybeans used, and the way in which they are prepared, tofu can range from meaty and firm to refined and runny, and can be eaten in an endless array of sweet and savoury dishes, raw, baked, boiled and stir-fried. My personal favourite is the creamy curd from Kyoto.

Tofu has cardiovascular benefits, is high in protein, iron, calcium, copper, selenium and magnesium. It helps in preventing diabetes and cancers, and is even better for you than consuming soy in general as it is made by boiling and curdling soybean curd, which leads to even more antioxidant and free-radical scavenging health benefits. It is also completely vegan and free of animal fats, and because it is a protein it fills you up and helps you maintain energy levels.

Of course, like most foods, tofu can be enjoyed as a less healthy snack – particularly at Nikishi market in Kyoto where I grew up, where soymilk doughnuts (although, still healthier than the bread-like variety) and whipped *sofuto kureem* ice cream (soft-serve ice cream) are specialities.

STEAMED TOFU WITH SPICY PORK

This has to be one of the easiest dishes to cook in this book. Tofu is an ingredient that can take big, strong flavours and it is eaten and enjoyed all over Japan. You can add any toppings you like: treat it like jacket potato, but a healthier version!

SERVES 4

300g silken tofu
1 tablespoon miso paste
1 teaspoon chilli paste
1 tablespoon soy sauce
2 teaspoons cooking oil
150g minced pork
1 tablespoon mirin
2 tablespoons sake
1 teaspoon sugar
coriander or shiso leaves, roughly
    chopped
2 spring onions, finely chopped
2 teaspoons sesame oil

Place the tofu in a steamer and steam for 12–15 minutes, or until the centre of the tofu is hot. Alternatively, place on an ovenproof plate in the microwave, cover with cling film and cook using medium-low heat for 3–4 minutes (900 watts).

Mix the miso and chilli pastes with the soy sauce in a small bowl and set aside.

Heat the cooking oil in a frying pan until very hot, add the pork and fry for 1 minute, until pale. Add the mirin and sake, and stir-fry for 30 seconds. Stir in the miso and soy sauce mixture, add the sugar, and cook for a further minute. Turn off the heat.

Lay the tofu on kitchen paper and pat dry, then place it on a serving dish. Sprinkle over half the chopped coriander or shiso and the spring onion, and then tumble the pork over the top. Add the sesame oil and sprinkle with the remaining coriander, or shiso, and spring onion.

Note: Feel free to use chicken, prawns or scallops instead of pork. For a vegetarian option, mushrooms and sweetcorn work very well.

CHAKIN TOFU
IN GINGER BROTH

This is a dish for true tofu lovers. It's worth obtaining high-quality tofu as it really makes a difference. A very virtuous bowl, I feel very clean and fresh eating this.

SERVES 4

400g block good-quality firm tofu
2g dried wakame seaweed
200g minced chicken breast
1 teaspoon soy sauce
1 tablespoon sake
1 egg white
50g carrot, finely chopped
3 spring onions, finely chopped
2 teaspoons finely grated ginger
1 tablespoon cornflour
1 teaspoon baking powder
salt and ground white pepper

For the ginger broth
750ml dashi stock (page 28) or 2
　　teaspoons instant dashi powder
　　mixed with water
3 tablespoons soy sauce
2 tablespoons sake
2 tablespoons mirin
4 shallots, thinly sliced
1 tablespoon cornflour mixed with 1
　　tablespoon water

Wrap the tofu in muslin cloth and squeeze out as much of the water as you can. Chop roughly and set aside.

Soak the dried wakame in a bowl of cold water for 5–10 minutes. Drain and squeeze out the water, then chop finely.

Combine the chicken with the soy sauce, sake and egg white in a large bowl, mixing well with your hands. Add the tofu, carrot, spring onions, 1 teaspoon grated ginger, wakame, cornflour, baking powder, salt and white pepper. Carry on mixing well until everything is combined.

Line a small rice bowl with a sheet of cling film and scoop a quarter of the tofu mixture into the bowl. Wrap the tofu firmly with cling film as if you are making a small parcel. Secure the top with a rubber band and repeat to make 3 more parcels. Place the parcels in a steamer and steam for about 20 minutes on medium-low heat.

Whilst the parcels are steaming, make the broth. Heat the dashi stock in a saucepan, add the soy sauce, sake and mirin, and simmer for 3–4 minutes. Add the shallots and season with salt and white pepper, and let it boil for 2 minutes. Pour in the cornflour mixture and continue to cook, stirring all the time, for about 20 seconds or until the broth is thickened and shiny.

Remove the cling film from the tofu parcels and place each in individual bowls. Pour the broth over the top, and serve with the remaining grated ginger alongside.

PRAWN AND CHICKEN TOFU FRITTERS

In Japan *ganmodoki* is a traditional tofu fritter, normally simmered in broth with other ingredients. Here, I'm introducing a different way of enjoying it: with a ginger and daikon dipping sauce. All very authentic flavours.

SERVES 4 (MAKES 12)

400g firm tofu
60g raw prawns, deveined
60g minced chicken
½ tablespoon soy sauce
½ tablespoon mirin
½ tablespoon ginger juice
½ medium potato
pinch of salt
1 tablespoon cornflour
handful of rocket leaves
12 cooked and peeled chestnuts
3–4 tablespoons plain flour
1 lime, quartered, to serve

For the ginger and daikon radish dipping sauce
2 tablespoons rice vinegar
4 tablespoons soy sauce
1 tablespoon brown sugar
1 tablespoon grated ginger
120g grated daikon radish

Mix all the ingredients for the dipping sauce in a bowl and set aside for at least 30 minutes to infuse.

Press the tofu between 2 chopping boards, weighing the top one down with tins of beans, for 2 hours. Alternatively, cut the tofu into large cubes and blanch them for 1 minute, drain and leave to cool.

Finely chop or mince the prawns until you have a smooth texture. Combine the prawns with the chicken, soy sauce, mirin and ginger juice in a small bowl.

Peel and grate the potato, and then gently squeeze out the excess water. Break up the tofu using a fork and mix it with the potato along with the minced chicken and prawn mixture. Add the salt. If the mixture appears too sloppy add the cornflour to make it firmer. Tear the rocket into bite-sized pieces, keeping the soft part and discarding any hard stems. Add to the tofu mixture and roughly mix.

Wet your hands and scoop out a small handful of the tofu mixture and form into 8–12 patties or small burgers about 7cm in diameter. Take a patty and press your index finger into the centre, then put a chestnut into the groove. Cover and re-form the patty. Repeat with the remaining patties.

Heat the oil in a wok or large frying pan to 150°C/300°F. If you don't have a thermometer you can test if the oil is hot by dropping a cube of bread in and it should sizzle and brown within 1 minute. Dredge the patties in flour very lightly, and slide them into the hot oil. Deep-fry them for 2–3 minutes, then increase the heat to high (180°C/350°F) and fry for a further 1–2 minutes or until the fritters are crisp and light golden brown. Remove using a slotted spoon and allow them to drain for a few minutes on kitchen paper.

Cut each fritter in half and serve with the dipping sauce and lime on the side.

TOFU BURGERS WITH OROSHI TERIYAKI SAUCE

I didn't create this recipe for the sake of a vegetarian option to the normal burger. It's all about the balance of health and taste, using both tofu and beef. (There is however a vegetarian option at the bottom of this recipe.)

SERVES 4

2 tablespoons vegetable, sunflower
    or corn oil
1 onion, finely chopped
300g firm tofu
300g minced beef
1 large egg, beaten
1 tablespoon grated ginger
handful of coriander, finely chopped
20g panko breadcrumbs
1 teaspoon salt
½ teaspoon ground white pepper
steamed vegetables, or salad, to
    serve

For the oroshi teriyaki sauce
125ml teriyaki sauce (page 31)
1 tablespoon rice vinegar
200g daikon radish, grated
½ onion, grated

Combine all the ingredients for the oroshi teriyaki in a bowl and then put in the fridge for at least 1 hour to infuse.

Heat 1 tablespoon oil in a frying pan and fry the onion gently for 6–7 minutes, or until soft and transparent. Leave them to cool.

Wrap the tofu in muslin or kitchen towel and squeeze as much water out as you can. Alternatively, place on a chopping board lined with kitchen paper. Place another chopping board on top along with some weights (such as a couple of tins of beans to help weigh down the board) and leave to drain for a couple of hours. Remove the tofu and squeeze out any excess water using your hands. Crumble to form a minced meat consistency and put in a large bowl.

Add the minced beef, cooled onion, egg, grated ginger, chopped coriander, breadcrumbs, salt and pepper to the bowl with the tofu and mix well using your hands. The motion should be like kneading dough.

Next, shape the mixture into burgers. The Japanese method is to make slightly large, oval shapes. If you are serving them with burger buns, you may prefer to shape them into rounds.

Heat 1 tablespoon oil in a large frying pan over medium heat. Add the burgers and fry them for about 2 minutes, then turn the heat down to medium-low and flip the burgers over. Cook for a further 4–5 minutes, or until just cooked. To test, insert a skewer into the centre of the burger and the juices should run clear. If not, continue to cook for a couple more minutes and test again.

Serve the burgers with any steamed vegetables, mushrooms or salad with the oroshi teriyaki sauce on the side. They also go very well with plain rice.

Note: For a vegetarian alternative, use the same amount of cooked chickpeas and sweetcorn, roughly minced, instead of the beef. Blitz the chickpeas and sweetcorn with a few tablespoons of vegetable oil in a food processor until minced and double the quantity of ginger and coriander.

ASIAN TOFU DANGO SOUP

Tofu is not only eaten in Japan but also throughout Asia. If you enjoy spicy
South Asian flavours, try these succulent tofu balls.

SERVES 4

For the balls
400g firm tofu
200g minced pork
1 tablespoon sake
1 tablespoon fish sauce
½ teaspoon salt
½ teaspoon ground black pepper
1 large egg, beaten
2 tablespoons cornflour
2 tablespoons finely chopped spring
  onion

For the broth
2 tablespoons dried prawns
handful of coriander stalks
2–3 red chillies, thinly sliced
2–3 garlic cloves, thinly sliced
150g shiitake mushrooms, cut into
  bite-sized pieces
200g rice noodles or konnyaku
  noodles
3 tablespoons fish sauce
1 tablespoon soy sauce
2 teaspoons sugar
1 sheet kombu
2 tablespoons roasted sesame oil
2–3 tablespoons coriander leaves,
  finely chopped, to garnish
2 limes, cut into wedges, to serve

In a large saucepan, soak the dried prawns in 2 litres of water for about 1 hour.

Put in the coriander stalks and bring to the boil over high heat. Turn down the
heat and simmer for about 20 minutes.

To make the balls, wrap the tofu in muslin cloth and squeeze out as much excess
water as possible, breaking it up as you do so.

Put the tofu in a bowl and combine with the ingredients for the balls using your
hands as if kneading dough. Continue mixing and kneading until the mixture
becomes elastic in consistency.

Bring the broth to the boil, add the chillies, garlic, shiitake mushrooms,
noodles, fish sauce, soy sauce, sugar and kombu, and bring back to the boil.
Using a teaspoon, scoop the tofu mixture and form into small-sized meatballs.
Drop them into the broth and cook for about 3–4 minutes, or until the balls are
just cooked.

Pour the sesame oil into the pan, give it one quick stir, then turn off the heat.
Serve in individual bowls with a sprinkling of chopped coriander and lime
wedges on the side.

TOFU SESAME KATSU

Firm tofu is ideal, not to mention healthy, as crunchy katsu. The subtle flavour of tofu with sesame seeds and sansho crumbs is a beautiful combination. Although it's deep fried, it's so light.

SERVES 4

400–600g firm tofu

130g buckwheat flour

2 eggs

100g panko breadcrumbs

100g toasted and ground sesame
  seeds

2 teaspoons sansho pepper

oil, for deep-frying

few sprigs watercress, roughly
  chopped

4 radishes, thinly sliced

For the miso sesame dipping sauce

2 tablespoons miso paste

1 tablespoon tahini paste

1 tablespoon soy sauce

4 tablespoons mirin

2 teaspoons sugar

½ teaspoon instant dashi powder
  mixed with 2 tablespoons water

2 teaspoons sesame oil

4 tablespoons finely chopped spring
  onions

Cut the tofu into 2 chunks and then place on a chopping board lined with kitchen paper. Place another chopping board on top along with some weights (such as a couple of tins of beans to help weigh down the board) and leave to drain for 2 hours, or until the thickness of the tofu is reduced by about 30 per cent.

Meanwhile, make the sauce simply by mixing all the ingredients in a bowl. You may make the sauce up to a few hours in advance and keep it in the fridge – just make sure to take it out of the fridge at least 1 hour before serving to let it come to room temperature.

Put the flour on a plate and beat the eggs in a shallow bowl. Press and rub the panko breadcrumbs between your hands to make them finer and then mix them with the ground sesame seeds and sansho pepper on a large plate.

Remove the kitchen paper from the tofu and pat the chunks dry with fresh kitchen paper. Dust the tofu all over with flour, dip into the beaten egg and then coat generously and thickly in the panko mixture.

Pour in enough oil to come at least 5cm up the sides of a wok or saucepan and heat to 160°C/320°F. Test the temperature by dropping a single crumb into the oil. If the crumb bounces back up straight away, the oil is ready. Carefully slide the tofu chunks into the hot oil and deep-fry until the chunks are golden brown, turning a few times during frying. Remove from the heat using a slotted spoon and drain on kitchen paper.

Arrange the watercress and sliced radish on a plate. Slice the tofu katsu into about 2.5cm thick pieces and put alongside the salad. Serve with the dipping sauce.

AGEDASHI TOFU IN PRAWN BROTH

Agedashi tofu is one of the most popular tofu dishes amongst Westerners.
I have created a more luxurious recipe with a thick prawn broth.

SERVES 4

400g firm or silken tofu

50g cornflour, for dusting

1 litre sunflower or vegetable oil, for deep-frying

handful of watercress, to garnish

For the prawn broth

3 tablespoons sake

160g raw prawns, deveined and roughly chopped

500ml dashi stock (page 28) or 1½ teaspoons instant dashi powder mixed with water

2 tablespoons mirin

3 tablespoons soy sauce

pinch of salt

1½ tablespoons cornflour mixed with equal amount of water

50g ginger, thinly sliced into matchsticks

Cut the tofu into 4 pieces and then place them on a chopping board lined with kitchen paper. Place another chopping board on top along with some weights (such as a couple of tins of beans to help weigh down the board) and leave to drain for a couple of hours.

Cut each chunk of tofu in half, leaving 8 squares altogether. Heat the oil in a wok or large wide frying pan to 170°C/340°F, making sure all of the tofu will be covered in the oil. Pat the tofu dry with kitchen paper and dredge each square with cornflour. Carefully slide the tofu into the hot oil and deep-fry for 2–3 minutes, turning all the time until golden brown. Take them out using a slotted spoon and drain on kitchen paper.

To make the broth heat the sake in a saucepan and then add the prawns. Cook for about 1 minute over medium-high heat, then pour in the dashi stock and bring to the boil. Stir in the mirin, soy sauce and salt and taste to adjust the seasoning. Reduce the heat to medium and simmer for 3–4 minutes.

Turn up the heat under the broth, bring to the boil, then pour the cornflour mixture into the pan, stirring well as you do so. Cook for about 5 minutes until the broth has thickened then turn off the heat. Just before serving, add the thinly sliced ginger.

Place 2 tofu squares in individual bowls and then pour the prawn broth on top. Garnish with the watercress and serve.

STEAMED TOFU WITH SCALLOPS AND SHIITAKE MUSHROOMS

The silken tofu, scallops and shiitake mushrooms complement each other extremely well. It's probably the best harmonised dish of any in this book. A little touch of soy sauce and sesame oil is all it needs.

SERVES 4

4 medium-sized dried shiitake
   mushrooms
½ teaspoon sugar
400g firm tofu
160g scallops, cut into 1cm cubes
1 large egg
1 tablespoon cornflour
pinch of baking powder
2 tablespoons sesame oil
1½ tablespoons soy sauce
2 teaspoons mirin
handful of coriander leaves, roughly
   chopped, to serve
handful of chives, chopped, to serve
salt and ground white pepper

Soak the dried shiitake mushrooms in a bowl of water with the sugar for at least 1 hour. Drain and squeeze the excess water from the mushrooms. Cut off and discard the stalks and chop the caps finely. Set aside.

Wrap the tofu with muslin cloth and firmly squeeze as much water out as possible. Transfer the tofu, breaking it up, to a bowl, then add the chopped shiitake mushrooms and scallops. Gently mix together.

Beat the egg in a small bowl with a pinch of salt and ground white pepper, then mix this into the tofu mixture. Add the cornflour and baking powder and gently combine. Transfer the tofu mixture to a large heatproof bowl.

Place the whole bowl in a large streamer and steam over medium-low heat for 20–30 minutes, until set. (The steaming time will depend on the size of the bowl.) After 20 minutes, insert a skewer into the centre and if the liquid comes out clear it is cooked. If not, steam for a few minutes more.

Heat the sesame oil, soy sauce and mirin in a small saucepan and simmer for 1–2 minutes. To serve, pour the sauce over the tofu and scatter with chopped coriander and chives.

AUBERGINE STEAK WITH SMOKED TOFU AND SHIITAKE MUSHROOMS

This is a very satisfying vegan main dish. The three main ingredients of aubergine, smoked tofu and shiitake mushroom marry together perfectly.

SERVES 4

20g dried shiitake mushrooms
1 large aubergine
3 tablespoons vegetable oil
80g sugar snap peas
3 tablespoons white miso paste
3 tablespoons soy sauce
3 tablespoons mirin
1 tablespoon sugar
1 tablespoon rice vinegar
1 teaspoon grated ginger
120g smoked tofu, cubed
1 tablespoon mixed black and white
    sesame seeds

Soak the shiitake mushrooms in a bowl of water for about 2 hours. Drain and squeeze out the excess water, and thinly slice. Set aside.

Slice the aubergine into quarters lengthways to get large flat 'steaks'. Trim the ends.

Heat 2 tablespoons oil in a large frying pan over medium heat. Once the pan is hot, lay the sliced aubergines in the pan, lower the heat and fry for 6–7 minutes, depending on the thickness of the aubergines. Turn the aubergine steaks over and cook for a further 4–5 minutes.

While the aubergines are cooking, slice the sugar snap peas thinly on the diagonal.

Combine the miso, soy sauce, mirin, sugar, rice vinegar, grated ginger and 3 tablespoons water in a bowl and set aside.

In a separate frying pan, heat the remaining 1 tablespoon oil and then add the sugar snap peas and mushrooms, and stir-fry over medium heat for 2 minutes. Stir in the smoked tofu and cook for a further minute, then turn up the heat and add the miso mixture. Continue to cook over high heat for 1 minute, then take off the heat.

To serve, arrange the aubergine steaks on individual plates, tumble the mushroom and tofu mixture on top and sprinkle with the sesame seeds.

SAVOURY STEAMED EGG CUSTARD

Chawanmushi, or steamed egg custard, is an authentic and refined Japanese dish. Because of the custard-like texture, it can be a little strange that it is a savoury dish for Western tastes, but I'm showing you the traditional version as its best.

SERVES 4

2 medium dried shiitake mushrooms
¼ teaspoon sugar
100g spinach
450ml cold dashi stock (page 28)
2 tablespoons soy sauce
1 teaspoon sake
1 tablespoon mirin
4 eggs, lightly beaten
100g small fresh prawns
4 cooked ginko nuts, chestnuts or lily
   bulbs, optional
salt

Soak the dried mushrooms in a bowl of warm water with the sugar (the addition of sugar makes the dried mushroom plump up faster) for at least 1 hour. Cut the stalks off and discard them, and slice the caps thinly.

Bring a saucepan of water to the boil with a pinch of salt and blanch the spinach leaves for 10 seconds. Drain under cold water and squeeze out as much excess water as possible.

Combine the dashi stock, soy sauce, sake, mirin and pinch of salt in a large bowl. Add the eggs and then strain through a fine sieve into a large jug to make it easier to pour into individual cups.

Divide the prawns, mushrooms, spinach and ginko nuts (if using) between 4 individual *chawanmushi* cups, ramekins or small soup bowls. Pour the egg mixture into the cups, allowing room for the egg mixture to rise when cooked.

Place in a steamer allowing enough space for steam to circulate between the cups. Lay a sheet of muslin cloth between the lid and the steamer (this will prevent the condensation from dripping into the egg mixture and changing its delicate texture). Bring the water in the steamer to a simmer, reduce the heat, then steam gently on medium-low heat for 15–20 minutes, or until the custard is just set but not firm. The steaming time will depend on the depth of your cups.

When they are ready, turn off the heat, leave them to sit for a few minutes, then place on saucers to serve. Alternatively, the custard can be served chilled in the summer.

JAPANESE SWEET OMELETTE

This is a versatile omelette, and often used for sushi recipes or as a side dish. It can also be made into a more interesting dish with the addition of various vegetables (page 179).

SERVES 4

For the omelette
vegetable or sunflower oil, for frying
4 eggs, beaten
1 teaspoon instant dashi powder
1½ tablespoons mirin
2 teaspoons caster sugar
½ teaspoons soy sauce
pinch of salt

To serve
grated daikon radish
soy sauce

Mix all the ingredients for the omelette in a large jug and stir well.

Heat an omelette pan over medium heat. Dip kitchen paper in a little vegetable or sunflower oil and wipe the pan to grease it or drizzle a little oil into the pan, tilting the pan to spread the oil evenly.

Pour in about 15 per cent of the egg mixture. Tilt the pan to coat the base evenly with the egg mixture. When the egg starts to set, roll it up towards you using chopsticks or a spatula. Make sure you roll it while the surface of the egg is still wet otherwise the omelette won't stick.

Keeping the rolled omelette in the pan, push it back to the furthest side from you. Grease the empty part of the pan again and pour another 10 per cent of the egg mixture into the pan at the empty side. Lift up the first roll with chopsticks, and let the egg mixture run underneath. When it looks half set, roll the omelette around the first roll to make a single roll with several layers.

Repeat this process, making more omelettes to roll around the first 2 rolls, until you have used up half of the egg mixture, then start again. You will end up with 2 multi-layered omelette rolls. Move the omelette rolls gently onto a sushi mat, place a plate on top to weigh it down and leave to stand for 10 minutes.

Slice the omelettes into 2.5cm thick slices and garnish with grated daikon and serve with soy sauce for dipping.

Note: Try mixing finely chopped smoked ham, spring onions or any ingredients you like to the egg mixture. Just make sure they are chopped very finely or it will make the omelette difficult to roll.

VEGETABLE TAMAGO-YAKI WITH THICK PONZU SAUCE

The original dish is known as 'Kani-Tama' in Japan, which means crab and egg. As a healthy option I'm using lots of vegetables, which also looks very pretty. It's easy to obtain all the ingredients and quick to cook!

SERVES 4

1 tablespoon sesame oil, plus extra
100g green beans, cut thinly into diagonal slices
1 medium carrot, cut into thin sticks
100g shiitake mushrooms, thinly sliced
4 stalks spring onion, finely chopped
1 teaspoon soy sauce
1 teaspoon mirin
6 eggs
½ teaspoon salt
½ teaspoon white pepper
1 tablespoon grated daikon, optional
1 teaspoon grated ginger, optional

For the ponzu sauce
1 teaspoon instant dashi powder
4 tablespoons soy sauce
2 tablespoons rice vinegar
2 tablespoons mirin
1 tablespoon sugar
1 teaspoon cornflour mixed with 80ml of water

Heat all the ingredients for ponzu sauce except for the cornflour in a small saucepan. Once it comes to a boil turn the heat off and set aside.

Heat a frying pan on medium heat and then add sesame oil and fry all the vegetables with the soy sauce and mirin until the vegetables soften and almost all the liquid has evaporated. Transfer them onto a plate to cool.

Crack the eggs into a bowl, add salt and pepper and whisk them well. Stir in the cooked vegetables.

Heat a large frying pan or omelette pan over a medium heat, add a little oil to the pan and tilt the pan left and right to spread the oil evenly. Pour in about 15 per cent of the egg and vegetable mixture and tilt the pan a little to make an even layer of egg and coat the inside of the pan, making sure all the vegetables are evenly spread out. When the egg starts to set, roll it up towards you with chopsticks or a spatula. Make sure you roll it while the surface of the egg is still wet or the layers won't stick.

Keeping the rolled omelette in the pan, push it back to the furthest side from you. Grease the empty part of the pan again and pour another 10 per cent of the egg mixture into the empty side of the pan. Lift up the first roll with chopsticks and let the egg mixture run underneath. When it looks half set, roll this second omelette around the first roll to make a single roll with many layers.

Repeat this process, making more omelettes to roll around the first 2 rolls until you have used up half the egg mixture. Move the roll gently on to a bamboo sushi mat and leave to stand rolled up for 5 minutes. Repeat the whole process again to make another roll with the remaining egg mixture.

Place the grated daikon on a small condiments plate and then top with grated ginger. Cut the rolled omelettes into inch-thick slices and plate up. Quickly reheat the ponzu sauce, pour in the cornflour and water mixture, stirring all the time, until the sauce thickens. Drizzle the sauce over the omelette slices and serve with the grated daikon and ginger.

NABE

Nabemono, or *nabe*, is a hearty hotpot dish in which seafood, meat or vegetables are cooked in a bubbling cauldron, a *donabe* (clay pot). These piping-hot broths are a wintertime favourite in Japan, perhaps a Japanese replacement for hearty British stews or Alpine fondue – although rather more healthy.

Nabe stews are eaten at home, with the quintessential image of a Japanese family sitting around their communal stew pot, and are served in restaurants where diners all share in the cooking too. The broth sits in the middle of the table atop a gas or charcoal *hibachi* burner and diners are given a tray of raw meat, seafood, mushrooms and crisp vegetables to add the pot, before the more delicate foods such as tofu and chrysanthemum leaves are offered.

Unlike Western stews, *nabe* is cooked quickly so that the ingredients retain their tastes, textures and nutrition; once cooked, diners tuck in with an oversized pair of chopsticks, plucking out pieces of cooked fish or vegetable, and at the end of the meal rice or noodles are added to the pot to absorb the remaining stock that will have absorbed a huge amount of vitamins and minerals.

While typical ingredients include *negi* (Japanese leek) and *hakusai* (Chinese cabbage), there are many regional varieties such as beef *sukiyaki* where ingredients are simmered in a sweet soy sauce and dipped into raw beaten egg before being eaten; *shabu-shabu* where the bite-sized pieces are dipped into a ponzu citrus sauce before being eaten; or even *yosenabe* – an 'anything goes' hotpot. Recognising the health benefits of *nabe*, Japanese restaurants have recently gone so far as developing the '*bijin*' or 'beauty *nabe*', which contains a chicken bone broth to improve skin collagen, as well as fresh seafood, various seaweeds and organic vegetables.

Nabe is a wonderfully warming yet extremely healthy dish. You can add any Japanese superfood you like, or omit all dairy or wheat, and because it is traditional to consume the *nabe* stock too, absolutely no nutrition is lost.

TRADITIONAL AND REGIONAL NABE SELECTION

Nabe is a very popular dish to cook at home, enjoyed especially in winter served fondue style, which is sociable, warming and fun. You can create your own *nabe* easily using your favourite ingredients, I've suggested some below.

For Ishikari Nabe

400g salmon, cut into large pieces

200g tofu, silken or firm depending on preference, cut into large pieces

10cm gobo burdock root, shredded, optional

2 medium carrots, sliced at an angle into 5mm-thick pieces

2 medium potatoes, sliced into 7mm-thick pieces

2 leeks, sliced at an angle into 1cm-thick pieces

½ Chinese cabbage, roughly chopped

200–300g *shungiku* (chrysanthemum leaves), bottom hard part removed, roughly chopped

100g konnyaku (or shirataki) noodles, drained

200g enoki or shimeji mushrooms

For the Ishikari Nabe broth

1.5 litres vegetarian stock (page 28)

3 tablespoon sake

50g *sakekasu* sake lees (hard/pressed type)

80–90g miso

40g butter, optional

For Mizutaki Nabe

4 chicken thighs (boneless, skinless), each cut into 4 pieces

1 bunch of *shungiku* (chrysanthemum leaves), bottom hard part removed, roughly chopped

200g tofu, silken or firm depending on preference, cut into large bite-sized pieces, approx. 1-inch cubes

½ Chinese cabbage, roughly chopped

8 shiitake mushrooms

125g enoki or oyster mushrooms

For the Mizutaki Nabe broth

1.5 litres dashi stock (page 28)

20g kombu

200ml sake

120ml soy sauce

60ml mirin

pinch of salt

For Yose Nabe

4 scallops

4 shrimps

1 leek, roughly chopped

large bunch of enoki mushrooms

4 shiitake mushrooms

generous bunch of *shungiku* (chrysanthemum leaves), bottom hard part removed, roughly chopped

200g tofu, silken or firm depending on preference, cut into large bite-sized pieces, approx. 1-inch cubes

½ Chinese cabbage, roughly chopped

For the Yose Nabe broth

1.5 litres dashi stock (page 28)

20g kombu

200ml sake

120ml soy sauce

60ml mirin

pinch of salt

Making *nabe* is incredibly simple. Basically you boil the broth and add everything into the a large frying pan or Japanese hotpot (*nabe*) and eat as it cooks.

Ponzu sauce (page 179) is the most popular dipping sauce for vegetable and seafood-based *nabe*. At the end, rice or noodles are often added to the broth, which has soaked up all the flavour from the main ingredients.

SUKIYAKI NABE

This traditional *nabe* (hotpot) has been around for years and is still extremely popular. Using raw egg as a dipping sauce may not be your cup of tea but it's worth a try. Just make sure to use the best quality eggs and beef you can find.

SERVES 4

200g shirataki noodles

4 free-range organic eggs

2 tablespoons oil, for frying

600g beef loin or rib-eye steak, sliced very thinly (or chicken)

1 onion, sliced into chunks

2 leeks, roughly chopped

½ head Chinese cabbage, cut into chunks

300g *shungiku* (chrysanthemum flowers, available at Asian supermarkets)

8 shiitake mushrooms

1 bunch of enoki mushrooms

300g firm tofu, cubed

400g cooked udon noodles, optional

For the sukiyaki cooking broth

160ml soy sauce

120ml mirin

4 tablespoons sake

3 tablespoons sugar

Bring a pan of water to the boil and cook the shirataki noodles according to the packet instructions. Drain and rinse. If the noodles are very long, lay them on a chopping board and cut them into 10cm lengths.

In a bowl, combine the ingredients for the cooking broth with 250ml water. Set aside.

Have ready your serving bowls. Each person will have one egg each and will crack in their own egg in their bowl and stir through with chopsticks.

Heat a large heavy frying pan or Japanese hotpot (*nabe*) and add a little oil (traditionally this would be cooked at the table). Add 4 slices of beef. Quickly pour the cooking broth into the pan and add half of the vegetables, the tofu and the shirataki noodles. Cover with a lid and cook for 2 minutes, then as you eat, dip into the beaten egg dipping sauce.

When the first batch of ingredients have been cooked, add the remaining ingredients and repeat until done. If there is any leftover broth in the pan, add the udon noodles and cook them for a couple of minutes or until they soak up the liquid and serve as the next course.

SHABU SHABU NABE

Wagyu beef is known for its beautiful marbling and melt-in-the-mouth texture. Slicing it very thinly and searing it only briefly to retain the sweet juicy flavours is a great way to enjoy this quality beef. All you need is a delicious dipping sauce to go with it.

SERVES 4

300g firm tofu

200g shirataki or konnyaku noodles

600g finely sliced wagyu beef or finely sliced pork

200g mizuna leaves (or watercress or spinach)

200g leeks, roughly chopped

300g Chinese cabbage, chopped into bite-sized chunks

200g pak choi

2 litres dashi stock (page 28) or 3–4 teaspoons instant dashi powder mixed with water

300–400g cooked short-grain rice

2 eggs

2 tablespoons chopped spring onions, to serve

For the sesame dipping sauce

6 tablespoons tahini paste

3 tablespoons soy sauce

1 tablespoon rice vinegar

1 tablespoon caster sugar

1 tablespoon water

For the ponzu dipping sauce

5 tablespoons yuzu, lime or lemon juice

3 tablespoons mirin

8 tablespoons soy sauce

1 teaspoon instant dashi powder

1 teaspoon caster sugar

Drain and wrap the tofu with kitchen paper. Place the tofu on a chopping board with another chopping board on top and weigh down with a couple of tins of beans to remove the excess water from the tofu. Leave it sit for 2 hours then remove the tofu and cut it into large, bite-sized pieces.

Bring a pan of water to the boil and cook the noodles according to the packet instructions. Drain the noodles and rinse them under cold, running water.

Arrange the meat, vegetables, tofu and cooked noodles attractively on a large serving platter, keeping the different ingredients separate.

Prepare the 2 different dipping sauces by mixing all the ingredients together.

Heat the dashi stock in a large casserole dish or Japanese hotpot (*nabe*) and bring to the boil. Add a quarter of the vegetables, tofu and noodles. Bring the stock back to the boil and cook the vegetables for a few minutes. Use chopsticks to dip the meat, slice by slice, in the stock, swirling it around like fish swimming, until it is cooked to your liking – about 10–20 seconds. Finally, shake off any excess stock and dip the meat into the dipping sauces.

Repeat this process until all the vegetables and meat are done. Turn up the heat and reboil the stock, then add the rice. Simmer for about 10 minutes, until the rice has soaked up half of the stock and is plump and soft.

Beat the eggs and pour them all over the rice and immediately take off the heat. The eggs will cook naturally in the residual heat of the casserole. Sprinkle with the chopped spring onions, divide the rice between individual bowls and serve with the vegetables to complete the meal.

SOY MILK AND CHILLI NABE

This is an unconventional *nabe* as the stock is not the usual clear fish stock or kombu stock. The use of soy milk makes it creamier and richer than traditional *nabes*, and the chilli paste keeps you warm on a cold winter night.

SERVES 4

400g pork loin or belly, very thinly
    sliced
half Chinese cabbage, roughly
    chopped
1 bunch spinach, roughly 100g
1 stalk of leek, sliced
1 pack of oyster mushrooms, roughly
    125g
100g bean sprouts
300g firm tofu
2 squares of Mochi (white sticky rice)

For the broth
1.5 litre vegetarian stock (page 28)
250–350ml soy milk, unsweetened
4–6 tablespoons soy sauce
4 tablespoons mirin
1–2 tablespoons chilli paste
½ teaspoon salt

In a large heavy frying pan or Japanese hotpot (*nabe*), combine the ingredients for the nabe stock. Bring to the boil.

Add half of the slices of pork to the broth, along with half of the vegetables, the tofu and the Mochi. Cover with a lid and cook for 8–10 minutes, and then serve straight from the dish.

When the first batch of ingredients have been cooked, add the remaining ingredients and repeat until done.

MONKFISH NABE

This is my version of traditional *anko nabe*. It's the perfect winter one-pot dish, full of protein and vegetables. The combination of miso and chilli bean paste makes this dish unique and very tasty.

SERVES 4

200g monkfish liver, cut into bite-
   sized chunks
2 litres vegetarian stock (page 28) or
   instant vegetarian dashi powder
   mixed with water
8 small new potatoes, scrubbed
200g firm tofu, cut into 5cm cubes
1 large carrot, cut into 4 on the
   diagonal
2 leeks, cut into 2.5cm slices
200g shimeji mushrooms, torn into
   chunks
4 tablespoons miso paste
1–2 teaspoons Chinese chilli bean
   paste
125ml sake
125ml mirin
1 tablespoon soy sauce
600g monkfish tail, cut into 5cm
   cubes
seven spice powder
salt

Sprinkle the monkfish liver with a little salt and set aside for 5–10 minutes.

Put the vegetarian stock and potatoes in a flameproof casserole dish or Japanese hotpot (*nabe*) and cook with the lid on for 4–5 minutes, or until the potatoes are *al dente*.

Put the remaining ingredients into the dish (or *nabe*) except the monkfish, liver and seven spice powder. Cover and then cook for 4–5 minutes.

Add the monkfish and liver, replace the lid and then cook for a further 3–4 minutes. Serve the *nabe* dish at the table for everyone to eat from with the seven spice powder on the side.

JAPANESE POT-AU-FEU

This is the perfect dish for a cold winter's dinner. I always describe *oden* as Japanese *pot-au-feu*. I'm using rather authentic ingredients here, all of which can be obtained at good Japanese supermarkets, but as long as you have the good broth, you can use any ingredients you like.

SERVES 4

2 litres dashi stock (page 28)

few kombu sheets cut into 2-inch pieces

½ daikon radish, peeled and cut into 2cm thick rounds

2 medium potatoes, cut into bite-sized pieces

200g octopus or squid tentacles, cut into bite-sized pieces

4 hard-boiled eggs, peeled

1 konnyaku cake (yam starch), cut into large triangles

2 deep-fried tofu sheets, cut into triangles or 6 small deep-fried tofu cubes, blanched

4 fish cakes, such as *chikuwa*, *hanpen* and *satsumaage*, cut into large chunks

125ml soy sauce

4 tablespoons mirin

4 tablespoons sake

1 teaspoon sugar

Japanese mustard, to serve

Bring the dashi stock and kombu to the boil in a flameproof casserole dish. Add the daikon radish and cook over medium-low heat for 6–7 minutes. Add the potatoes and cook for a further 6–7 minutes.

Put the remaining ingredients in the casserole dish and bring to the boil. Immediately turn the heat down and simmer for about 30 minutes, covered, until the vegetables are tender. Check from time to time to make sure the ingredients are fully submerged in the broth. If not, add water and a little soy sauce and mirin to adjust the flavour to taste.

Once all the ingredients have absorbed the flavour from the broth, it's ready. Serve the casserole dish on the table with Japanese mustard on the side.

SUSHI

Of course one of the best-known rice dishes is sushi. In Japan, the most important part of sushi is the rice; we judge sushi restaurants first and foremost by the quality of their rice. In the Basics section (page 27), we looked at how to make perfect sushi rice, which should have just the right amount of stickiness and be neither *al dente* nor mushy, with sushi seasoning ideally folded in using a fan and sushi barrel (*Uchiwa*, *handai* and *hangiri*, see page 15). Sushi rice should be served very slightly lukewarm or at room temperature (refrigeration will cause it to turn chalky in texture) as in the best sushi restaurants and counters. The sushi rice should be beautifully soft and fresh-tasting.

My students, most of whom are non-Japanese and enjoy sushi from various shops and supermarkets in the UK, are often surprised by their first experience of authentic sushi. It tastes utterly different to anything you can find in the supermarket, and trust me is far less difficult to make than expected.

The history of Japan's most famous dish reaches back 1,800 years, not to Japan but in fact to China. Initially invented in the 2nd century AD, fish would be wrapped in rice and left to ferment so that it remained edible for months rather than days; then, in the 7th century, this practice reached Japan where the rice was eaten with the fish. It wasn't until the 17th century, however, that Tokyo chef Matsumoto Yoshiichi started to season the rice with rice vinegar, which sped up the fermentation process and allowed the dish to be eaten immediately. Following the popularity of the sushi roll, *nigiri*, a slice of fish, omelette or vegetable placed on top of a shaped mound of rice, appeared in the 19th century in what was the first emergence of sushi as fast food – made to order as you wait – which is now the most common type of sushi eaten in Japan. Meanwhile, the California roll was only invented very recently and is wrapped 'inside-out' with the rice on the outside to hide the *nori* seaweed, as it was initially seen as unappetising by Westerners!

Sushi pieces should always be bite-sized and beautifully presented, and as we all know, eating slowly reduces the amount of food that you eat as you will recognise when you are full. However, not only is eating sushi a way of staying slim, its ingredients are full of incredible benefits. First of all, the rice itself is a gluten-free and sustaining carbohydrate, and is seasoned with rice vinegar, which has antibacterial properties, aids digestion and lowers the risk of high blood pressure. Second, the black *nori* seaweed used to wrap the rice contains protein and is rich in iodine, niacin and vitamins A, B1, B2, B6 and C, and is even known to help prevent cholesterol deposits from building up in our blood vessels.

Sushi pieces may contain raw sashimi, seared or smoked fish, depending on your taste, all of which is equally high in protein. Although oily fish such as mackerel, sardine, salmon and tuna might appear to be fattier, the Japanese do prefer to use these varieties in their sushi as they provide the highest level of omega-3 fatty acids, which help to fight heart disease, the risk of strokes and arthritis.

In addition to its miracle ingredients, sushi is served with several superfood condiments: ginger, a natural antiseptic, which aids digestion and boosts the immune system; wasabi, rich in vitamin C and with antibacterial and antiseptic properties; and soy sauce, made from crushed soybeans which are full of protein, magnesium, potassium and iron. I often use tamari rather than soy sauce as it is gluten free and lower in salt, and one thing that I am always reminding my students is to dip the fish (not the rice) of their *nigiri* in the tamari, which limits the amount of salt you eat alongside your sushi as well as preserving the unique natural flavours of each sushi piece.

SALMON SPECIAL SCATTERED SUSHI – CHIRASHI

Scattered sushi is called *Chirashi Zushi* in Japanese, and the word *chirashi* means to scatter. This is the most popular type of sushi made at home in Japan as it is easy to make and you can scatter any ingredients you like over the top. Cooked and chopped vegetables or herbs can be mixed with sushi rice to enjoy the variety. Perfect sushi for a buffet meal!

SERVES 4

450g sushi rice (page 30)
2 teaspoons soy sauce, plus extra to
  serve
2 teaspoons mirin
120g salmon roe
120g sashimi salmon
120g slightly salted wild salmon
2 tablespoons toasted sesame seeds
7 sheets shiso leaves or watercress,
  torn or watercress leaves picked
1 dried nori sheet, thinly sliced
wasabi paste, to serve

For the omelette
1 tablespoon oil, for frying
2 free-range eggs, preferably organic
½ teaspoon instant dashi powder
1 teaspoon mirin
pinch of salt

Prepare and cook the rice according to the instructions on page 30.

To make the omelette, heat a little oil in a large frying pan. Beat the eggs, dashi powder, mirin and salt in a bowl, and pour half the mixture into the pan. Tilt the pan slightly so that the egg mixture covers the entire surface of the pan, making a thin layer. Cook over medium-high heat for 10 seconds then turn over and fry the remaining side for 5 seconds. Take out of the pan and set aside to cool. Repeat with the rest of the egg mixture, and then slice thinly. Set aside.

In a bowl, combine the soy sauce and mirin with the salmon roe and the sashimi salmon. Leave to marinate for at least 30 minutes and up to 2 hours in the fridge.

Preheat the grill to medium-high and then grill the salted salmon for 5 minutes. Turn over and cook for a further 2–3 minutes, or until just cooked. Remove and leave it to cool, then flake the salmon into large pieces.

Remove the sashimi salmon from the marinade and slice into small bite-sized pieces.

Gently mix the sushi rice, grilled salmon, sesame seeds, half the quantity of sliced omelette and half the shiso leaves or watercress until evenly combined. Gently fold through half the amount of salmon roe.

Spoon into a serving bowl, decorate with the sashimi salmon, remaining salmon roe and omelette, and scatter over the rest of the shiso or watercress on top. To serve, sprinkle with a little nori and have soy sauce and wasabi paste on the side for seasoning.

EEL AND AVOCADO ROLL

Once you master the skill of the inside-out roll, try this one; it's so pretty with the layers of avocados outside. Unagi eel and avocado is a beautifully rich combination and *tobiko* adds the nice crunch.

MAKES 2 ROLLS

1 ripe avocado
1 nori sheet
225g cooked sushi rice (page 30)
4 tablespoons black sesame seeds
2 tablespoons wasabi mayonnaise (page 47)
1 tablespoon *tobiko* (flying fish roe)
200–300g ready-cooked unagi eel, sliced
4 sticks of pickled daikon radish, cut into 1 × 10cm pieces
¼ cucumber, cut into matchsticks

Slice the avocado in half, remove the stone and slice the flesh into fine segments.

Cut the nori sheet in half and place one half on the sushi mat. Wet both hands and press a handful of sushi rice on top of the nori, spreading it out evenly.

Lay half the avocado in rows over the rice, making sure there are no gaps. Sprinkle a line of sesame seeds horizontally over the avocado, then cover with cling film. Place another sushi mat over the top. Lift the entire assembly and turn it over. Take the sushi mat on top (originally the bottom) off.

Dollop a line of the wasabi mayonnaise horizontally in the centre of the nori sheet, then top with the *tobiko* and lay half of the eel on top. Lay pickled radish and cucumber alongside the eel so that all the fillings sit nicely together at the centre of the nori sheet.

Using both hands, lift the end of the mat closest to you with your thumbs and index fingers. Carefully roll up the nori sheet (using the sushi mat as a guide), securing the fillings as you go, rolling towards the far side. Repeat using the second half of the nori sheet and remaining ingredients to make a second roll.

Take the cling film off and slice each roll into 8 pieces.

SALMON INSIDE OUT ROLL

This is an elegant looking and innovative roll for your dinner party. As salmon is the most loved fish in the UK, I promise this will be the most popular roll!

MAKES 2 ROLLS

100g salmon fillet, with skin on
2 tablespoons Japanese mayonnaise
2–3 spring onions, finely chopped
½ avocado
1 nori sheet
225g cooked sushi rice (page 39)
100g lightly smoked salmon or cured salmon, thinly sliced
2 medium-sized gherkins, thinly sliced
2 teaspoons white sesame seeds, to sprinkle
salt

For the dark dengaku miso
2½ teaspoons miso paste
1 tablespoon mirin
¾ teaspoon sugar

For the white dengaku miso
2½ teaspoons white miso paste
1 tablespoon mirin

First prepare the filling. Preheat the grill to medium-high. Lightly season the salmon fillet with salt and grill, skin-side down, for about 3 minutes. Turn it over and grill skin-side up for about 5 minutes, or until the skin is crisp but not burned. Remove and allow to cool enough to handle, remove the crisp skin and tear into a bowl. Shred the flesh into small pieces and put in a separate bowl with the mayonnaise and chopped spring onions. Mix well and set both bowls aside.

Remove the stone from the avocado and peel. Slice the flesh into thin segments.

Cut the nori sheet in half and place one half on the sushi mat. Dip your hands in cold water, shake off the excess, then scoop up half of the sushi rice. Spread the rice over the nori sheet, covering it evenly. Press the rice gently to smooth out the surface but do not use too much force. The thickness of the rice should be around 7mm.

Lay half the thinly sliced smoked or cured salmon evenly over the rice. Cover the surface with cling film and then place another sushi mat over the top and press it down lightly. Turn the whole thing over. Now you have the original sushi mat on the top, so remove this mat.

Lay half the salmon mayonnaise and chopped spring onion mixture over the nori sheet in a horizontal line across the centre followed by the salmon skin pieces, gherkins and avocado.

Using both hands, pick up the sides of the sushi mat and cling film closest to you with your index fingers and thumbs. Carefully roll up the nori sheet (using the mat and cling film as a guide), enclosing the filling (but not the cling film) inside the nori sheet as you roll, rolling away from you towards the far side. Try to roll as tightly as possible. Repeat with the remaining nori sheet and ingredients to make 2 rolls.

To make both the dengaku misos, simply mix the ingredients for each well until the sugar is completely dissolved. For the white dengaku miso, no sugar is needed as white miso is sweet.

Cut each roll into 8 pieces using a very sharp knife. When cutting, move the knife forward and backwards with a little pressure, holding the knife parallel to the chopping board. Never push the knife down or the rolls will be squashed.

Place a drop of the dark dengaku miso on top of each roll followed by a smaller drop of white dengaku miso. Lastly, sprinkle the sesame seeds on top of each sliced roll.

SOFT-SHELL CRAB ROLL

Everyone loves soft shell crab tempura, so why not make it a sushi roll? Chilli mayonnaise compliments the tempura and gives it a good punch. You could make these as prawn tempura rolls instead as prawns are easier to obtain.

MAKES 2 ROLLS

1 dried nori sheet
225g cooked sushi rice (page 30)
3 tablespoons *tobiko* (flying fish roe)
2 tablespoons chilli mayonnaise
3 teaspoons toasted white sesame
    seeds

For the soft-shell crab tempura
2 medium soft-shell crabs
240g tempura flour, plus extra to dust
250ml ice-cold water
1 litre vegetable oil, for deep-frying

First prepare the tempura. Cut each crab into 4 pieces, taking care not to squash them as the crabs are very soft. Rinse well.

Use chopsticks to roughly mix the tempura flour and ice-cold water in a bowl.

Pour enough oil in a wok or large frying pan to come about 5cm up the sides of the pan and heat to 170°C/340°F. Dust each piece of crab in tempura flour, allowing the excess to brush off, and then dip into the batter making sure to coat well.

Slowly lower the battered crab into the hot oil in batches, taking care to make the shape of the crab as neat and tidy as possible so it's easier to roll, and deep-fry for 1–2 minutes, or until the batter is lightly golden and crispy. Repeat with the remaining crab until done. Remove with a slotted spoon and set aside on kitchen paper to drain.

To assemble the crab roll, cut the nori sheet in half and place one half on the sushi mat.

Wet both hands and press a handful of sushi rice on top of the nori, spreading it out evenly. Spread half of the *tobiko* over the rice and then cover with cling film. Place another sushi mat over the top. Lift the entire assembly and turn it over. Take the sushi mat on top (originally the bottom) off.

Spread a tablespoon of chilli mayonnaise in the centre of the nori sheet and lay 1 tempura crab on top – let the legs poke out at both ends of the nori.

Using both hands, lift the end of the mat closest to you with your thumbs and index fingers. Carefully roll up the nori sheet (using the sushi mat as a guide), securing the fillings as you go, rolling towards the far side. Repeat with the second half of the nori sheet and remaining ingredients to make a second roll.

Take the cling film off and slice each roll into 8 pieces.

RICH VEGETARIAN ROLL

This is a 'must try' sushi roll. By using a soft cheese, although it is a vegetarian roll, it becomes succulently rich. Fusion can be very successful!

SERVES 4 (MAKES 2 ROLLS)

2 ripe tomatoes
1 dried nori sheet
225g cooked sushi rice (page 30)
1 tablespoon black sesame seeds
1 tablespoon toasted white sesame seeds
½ ripe avocado
60g soft cheese such as brie or camembert
1 roasted red pepper
¼ medium cucumber, cut into sticks

Bring a saucepan of water to the boil. Make a little criss-cross score at the base of the tomatoes, add them to the pan of boiling water and leave for 30 seconds. Drain and rinse under cold water. Peel off the skins, cut each tomato into quarters and remove the seeds.

Cut the nori sheet in half and place one half on the sushi mat. Wet both hands and press a handful of sushi rice on top of the nori, spreading it out evenly.

Mix the black and white sesame seeds together and then sprinkle them in a thin line on top of the rice.

Cover with a sheet of cling film, then place another sushi mat over the top. Lift and hold the entire assembly and turn it over. Take the sushi mat on top (originally the bottom) off.

Peel and remove the stone from the avocado and slice into ½cm slices. Arrange the avocado slices with the tomatoes, soft cheese, red pepper and cucumber sticks across the nori in a straight line.

Using both hands, lift the end of the mat closest to you with your thumbs and index fingers. Carefully roll up the nori sheet (using the sushi mat as a guide), securing the fillings as you go, rolling towards the far side. Make sure not to press too firmly otherwise you'll squash the tomatoes. Repeat the process with the other half of the nori sheet and remaining ingredients to make a second roll.

Take the cling film off and slice the rolls into 8 pieces.

VEGETARIAN HAND-MOULDED NIGIRIS

Nigiri is the most technical sushi to perfect. Raw fish topping is most often used in Japan, however I have created colourful and tasty vegetarian versions here for you to have a go at making.

HAND-MOULDED NIGIRI

SERVES 4 (MAKES 16 PIECES)

320g cooked sushi rice (page 30)
wasabi paste, to taste

Nigiri topping suggestions
1 roasted red or orange pepper, thinly
    sliced
½ avocado, destoned and thinly
    sliced
4 slices smoked tofu, cut into thin
    slices approx 5–7mm thick
Tamago-yaki (Japanese sweet
    rolled omelette) (page 177), sliced
    diagonally into 5mm thick pieces
20g pickled daikon radish, cut into
    thin matchsticks

For each piece of sushi, dip your leading hand in cold water, scoop up about a tablespoonful of sushi rice (each rice ball should weigh 15–20g), then gently but firmly mould the rice into a ball, making it slightly oval in shape. Do not squash the rice but make sure the grains stick together firmly. The size of the rice ball must be smaller than the toppings. Repeat with the remaining sushi rice to make about 16 rice balls.

Place the toppings of your choice on top of each rice ball. Lightly press them together as if you are wrapping the rice with the topping. The topping should be elegantly draped over the rice. Serve.

COURGETTE NIGIRI

SERVES 4 (MAKES 16 PIECES)

4 large baby courgettes or 1 courgette
1 red chilli, thinly sliced
½ teaspoon salt
125ml sushi vinegar
5g kombu sheet or ½ teaspoon
    kombu sprinkles
½ teaspoon instant dashi powder
16 nigiri rice balls (page 206)

Slice the baby courgettes diagonally and into long lengths. Put in a bowl with the chilli, salt, sushi vinegar and kombu sheet or sprinkles.

Mix the dashi powder with 125ml water and pour over the courgettes. Stir, then allow to pickle for at least 2 hours. Alternatively, make this the day before and keep in the fridge.

When ready to serve remove the courgette from the fridge and lightly press each slice on top of each rice ball. Serve.

SWEETCORN GUNKAN NIGIRI

SERVES 4 (MAKES 16 PIECES)

4 teaspoons tinned sweetcorn,
   drained
1 tablespoon chilli mayonnaise
3 nori sheets, cut into ribbons about
   18cm long and 4cm wide
16 nigiri rice balls (page 206)

Rinse the sweetcorn kernals and pat them dry with paper towels. Put the sweetcorn in a bowl with the mayonnaise and combine.

Wrap a nori strip around the outside of each rice ball, moulding into an oval shape like a battleship. Ensure that the top edge of the nori comes up a little higher than the top of the rice leaving enough room for your topping. Using a teaspoon, add the sweetcorn filling on the top of the nori 'battleship' and serve immediately.

CUCUMBER AND WAKAME GUNKAN NIGIRI

SERVES 4 (MAKES 16 PIECES)

½ cucumber
pinch of salt
5g dried wakame, soaked in water for
   10 minutes
1 teaspoon sushi vinegar
1 teaspoon white sesame seeds
½ teaspoon roasted sesame oil
3 nori sheets, cut into ribbons about
   18cm long and 4cm wide
16 nigiri rice balls (page 206)

Cut the cucumber to make rough 18cm barrels, then use a vegetable peeler to shave them, creating thick ribbons. Place in a bowl and sprinkle with the salt. Leave to macerate for 5 minutes, then pat dry using kitchen paper.

Squeeze excess water from the wakame and stir together with the sushi vinegar, sesame seeds and sesame oil.

Wrap a nori strip around the outside of each rice ball, moulding into an oval shape like a battleship. Ensure that the top edge of the nori comes up a little higher than the top of the rice leaving enough room for your topping. Using a teaspoon, spoon the cucumber and wakame filling on top of the nori 'battleship' and serve immediately.

SWEET

Sweets dishes may seem off-topic, but this is not a dieting book. Rather it is an introduction to the Japanese lifestyle and diet – which happens to be both delicious and extremely healthy – and the Japanese do eat desserts, albeit in small portions. The most traditional Japanese sweets include fresh and perishable *namagashi* and *higashi* candies, which are sculpted and carved like ornaments and served at tea ceremonies and celebrations.

As a child, my lasting memory of desserts is of moving to the living room after dinner and sitting together with light, refreshing sweets or seasonal fruits. My favourites were Japanese pears, crunchy and juicy like an apple but with a strong, sweet scent, hints of cinnamon and butterscotch, and ranging from pale yellow to caramel to russet red. In comparison to my tiny hands these fruits must have looked enormous.

Another fruit that remains in my mind is the Japanese strawberry: seeing boxes of them at the market delicately lined with tissue, each strawberry identical in shape and size, and shiny red. Recently in Japanese high-end department stores, I have seen strawberries almost the size of small apples; these are a delicacy and boast an unforgettable flavour. In fact, they are such a treat that at upmarket restaurants it is not uncommon to be given a single enormous strawberry as a dessert.

The Japanese seem to share the same love for fruit as the English, which translates into many different varieties of sweet foods. One of the most popular strawberry sweets is *ichigo daifuku*, essentially a whole strawberry encased in red bean paste and sweet *mochi* (pounded glutinous rice).

Another well-loved flavouring is *matcha* (green tea powder), which is becoming increasingly popular in the West. The Japanese have always used it in ice cream and simple pound cakes. I like to infuse *matcha* into soufflés, crème brûlées and tiramisu. For my *matcha* ice cream, I also like to incorporate soy milk to keep it light and use Japanese flavourings such as red bean, preserved cherry blossom, yuzu or sesame seeds. Like *matcha*, sesame is known as one of the world's healthiest foods, brimming with calcium, magnesium, iron, vitamin B1, zinc and fibre.

STRAWBERRY MOCHI

Daifuku mochi is a well-known authentic Japanese sweet of *mochi* (rice cake) stuffed with sweetened red bean paste. In recent years, it has become popular to stuff these with strawberries, making the dessert light and fresh. It's very delicious and surprisingly easy to make, too.

MAKES 8 MOCHI

180g azuki bean paste (page 214)
8 strawberries, hulled
120g *shiratamako* (glutinous/sweet rice flour) or 140g rice flour
40g sugar
100g potato starch or cornflour

Divide the red bean paste into 8 evenly sized balls – it will stick to your hands so wash and dry them completely each time you roll a ball. Flatten the balls a little.

Wrap the strawberries in the red bean paste, leaving the pointed tip of the strawberry uncovered.

In a heatproof glass bowl, mix the shiratamako or rice flour and sugar together well. Slowly add 120–140ml water, a third at a time, and stir until the mixture has reached a thick consistency.

Boil water in a steamer or large saucepan and steam the glass bowl with the flour mixture for 16–18 minutes with the lid of the steamer covered with a cloth.

Dust a clean surface with the potato starch or cornflour and tip the steamed flour mixture on top. Dust your hands with flour and, working quickly, divide the mixture into 8 balls.

Dust your hands with more potato starch or cornflour and flatten each of the balls into a rough 10cm disc. Shake off any excess potato starch and place a red bean strawberry in the centre of the disc, tip facing down. Bring the sides of the mochi in to cover the strawberry and use your thumb to hold the mochi upright. Pinch and twist to seal, making sure there are no gaps. Hold the mochi with both hands and form it into a nice round shape. Repeat the process for the remaining mochi.

Place the mochi on a chopping board and cut just before serving. These are best eaten on the day they are made but you could keep them in an airtight container or wrapped with cling film, either in a cool place or the fridge for up to 1 day.

BLACK SESAME AND CHERRY BLOSSOM TORTES

These are sublime mini-finger cakes with a light and nutty sponge. Filling them with salty, sweet and sour cherry blossom (*sakura*) cream not only looks stunning with the contrast of pink and black, but also produces a sensational flavour.

MAKES 4 TORTES

4 eggs
100g sugar
60g black sesame seeds
120g plain flour
15g melted butter, warm

For the cherry blossom cream filling

50g salt-preserved cherry blossoms (*sakura*, page 227), plus extra to decorate
180ml double cream
20g caster sugar
80g cherry jam

Preheat the oven to 180°C/350°F/Gas Mark 4. Using a standmixer or an electric whisk, beat the eggs and sugar until light and creamy.

Grind the sesame seeds using a mortar and pestle (or spice/coffee grinder) to a very fine powder.

Sift the flour and ground sesame into the egg and sugar mixture, and fold gently using a spatula. Gradually pour in the warmed melted butter, stirring with a wooden spoon to combine well.

Line a 33cm standard Swiss roll tin with baking parchment. Pour the mixture into the tin and bake for 12–15 minutes. Check if it is done by inserting a toothpick into the cake – if the toothpick comes out clean it is cooked.

Take the sponge out of the oven and leave it to cool for 10 minutes before gently removing it from the tin. Allow to cool completely.

While the cake is cooling, make the cherry cream. Briefly rinse the salted cherry blossoms, leaving a little of the salt on them. Chop them finely. Whisk the double cream with the sugar in a bowl until very thick. Mix in the finely chopped cherry blossoms and the cherry jam.

Use a sharp knife to cut the sponge into rectangles of 4cm × 10cm. Spread a generous amount of the cherry cream on top of one of the fingers, and add a second sponge finger to make a 'sandwich'. You should have 4 tortes. Finally, decorate each with a piece of the cherry blossom. This is best eaten on the day it is made or within a couple of days.

GREEN TEA DORAYAKI PANCAKES

Dorayaki makes a tasty teatime cake rather than after dinner dessert. However, simply adding *matcha* to the cake batter – and serving with cream – gives you a smarter-looking dish more appropriate to a dessert course. I've provided a recipe for the adzuki bean paste below, but alternatively, you can purchase tinned cooked red bean paste from Japanese or Asian supermarkets.

MAKES 8 SANDWICHES

3 eggs
150g sugar, plus 1 tablespoon sugar
180g self raising flour
1 teaspoon matcha powder
½ tablespoon glucose
½ teaspoon baking powder
2–3 tablespoons vegetable, corn or
    sunflower oil or butter
300ml double cream

For the adzuki bean paste
120g dried red beans
5–6 times as much water to red
    beans, around 600ml
120–150g sugar
1 teaspoon salt

First make the adzuki bean paste. Soak the red beans in a bowl of water overnight. The next day, drain and rinse the beans. Place the beans in a large saucepan with the water and bring to the boil for 1 minute. Turn the heat down to a simmer and cook for 1½–2 hours, skimming away any foam, or until the beans are tender. Add some water during this time, if necessary, to keep the beans completely submerged. Alternatively, cook for 20 minutes using a pressure cooker.

Add half the sugar and the salt to the beans and continue to cook over medium heat for a further 2 minutes. Stir in the remaining sugar and cook, uncovered, for another 45 minutes, until the liquid has evaporated and the mixture has become a thick paste. Allow to cool and then store in the fridge for up to 1 week or freeze until needed.

To make the pancakes whisk the eggs and 150g sugar until glossy in a large bowl. In a separate bowl, sift a third of the flour and matcha powder together. Repeat this 3 times so that the matcha and flour combine well and to aerate the mix.

Slowly add the sifted matcha flour into the egg mixture and fold in gently. In a separate bowl, stir together 85ml water and the glucose and then add the baking powder. Tip into the flour and egg mixture, then combine to form a smooth, thick batter. If the consistency is too stiff, add a little more water. Set aside for 15–20 minutes.

Heat a little oil or butter in a large frying pan over medium-low heat. Add ladlefuls of batter to the pan to make 8–10cm diameter rounds, fitting as many as you can fit in the pan. After a few minutes, bubbles should start appearing on the surface and the bottom will start to lightly brown. Flip over and cook the other side for a further 2–3 minutes, depending on the thickness of your pancakes.

Once both sides are cooked, take them out and repeat until all the batter is used. Set the pancakes aside to allow them to cool.

Meanwhile, whisk the cream with 1 tablespoon sugar until thick and holding its shape.

Spread one pancake with the adzuki bean paste and whipped cream. Sandwich another pancake on top. Repeat with the remaining pancakes and fillings. If you are making these in advance, spread the cream on just before serving.

Note: A variation on this recipe would be to use other seasonal, fresh fruits of your choice together with the adzuki bean paste and/or double cream.

MATCHA SOUFFLÉ

Matcha, a powdered green tea, is one of the most popular ingredients used in Japanese desserts. It goes extremely well with cream or white chocolate, and is traditionally paired with adzuki bean. Here, I've used it in a fluffy and sweet soufflé. I urge you to give it a try.

SERVES 4

15g unsalted butter, softened
8 tablespoons caster sugar
2 teaspoons matcha powder
8 egg whites
chocolate sauce (see page 229), to
    serve

For the crème pâtissière
4 egg yolks
70g caster sugar
20g cornflour
1½ teaspoons plain flour
375ml milk
1 vanilla pod, seeds scraped, or 1
    teaspoon vanilla extract
15g unsalted butter

First make the crème pâtissière. Whisk the egg yolks, sugar and flours in a bowl. Bring the milk and vanilla to the boil in a saucepan over medium heat. Slowly pour this into the bowl with the egg mixture, stirring constantly.

Return the mixture back into the pan and bring to the boil again, stirring constantly with a wooden spoon. Continue to cook for 2 minutes, stir in the butter, remove from the heat and pour into a bowl, whisking a few times to cool the mixture down to room temperature. Cover with cling film to prevent a skin forming and store in the fridge for up to 2 days.

When you are ready to make the soufflés, preheat the oven to 190°C/375°F/ Gas Mark 5. Grease four 300ml ramekins with the softened butter and sprinkle 1 tablespoon caster sugar into each ramekin, tilting each dish so to fully coat it with the sugar. Tap out any excess sugar.

Beat the matcha powder and crème pâtissière in a bowl using an electric whisk (or do this in a standmixer).

In a clean bowl, whisk the egg whites until soft peaks form. Gradually add the remaining 4 tablespoons sugar, whisking all the time, until the mixture becomes stiff and glossy.

Using a spatula or metal spoon, stir half of the whisked egg whites into the crème pâtissière to loosen it, then gently fold in the remaining whisked egg whites. Divide the mixture between the prepared ramekins and run your thumb around the inner rim of each ramekin (this will help the soufflé rise rather than collapse).

Arrange the ramekins in a roasting tin, then pour enough just-boiled water into the roasting tin to come two-thirds of the way up the sides of the ramekins. Place in the oven and cook the soufflés for 15–17 minutes, until well risen and slightly wobbly. To check if they are done, insert a skewer into the centre of one soufflé – it should come out slightly moist but not wet.

Once done, remove from the oven and using a tea towel, very carefully take the soufflés out of the tin without touching the tops. Serve them immediately with warm chocolate sauce on the side.

YUZU POSSET WITH SESAME SHORTBREAD

Yuzu is a Japanese citrus fruit somewhere between a lemon, a lime and a mandarin. This recipe is my first Japanese-English fusion dessert, and it really is extremely easy to make. The light sesame shortbread is a perfect accompaniment to the creamy posset.

SERVES 4–6, DEPENDING ON THE SIZE OF SERVING BOWLS

400ml double cream
135g caster sugar
50ml yuzu juice
1 tablespoon finely grated mandarin or lemon zest, plus extra to serve

For the sesame shortbread
150g unsalted butter, diced
80g golden caster sugar
170g plain flour
40g extra fine black sesame seed powder
pinch of salt

First make the posset. Gently heat the cream and sugar in a large saucepan, stirring until the sugar has melted. Bring to a simmer and let it bubble for 1 minute.

Turn off the heat and stir in the yuzu juice and mandarin zest. Divide the mixture between 4 ramekins or small bowls and allow to cool to room temperature. Cover with cling film and chill for at least 3 hours, or up to 24 hours.

To make the sesame shortbread, beat the butter and 70g caster sugar in a food processor (or standmixer) until smooth and pale. Add the flour, black sesame powder and a pinch of salt, then mix again until combined.

Tip into a 16cm x 25cm baking tray and use your hands to spread the mixture out roughly. Cover with cling film and smooth over the surface until there are no wrinkles. Chill in the fridge for at least 30 minutes.

Preheat the oven to 180°C/350°F/Gas Mark 4. Remove the cling film from the shortbread and sprinkle with the remaining 10g sugar. Bake for 20–25 minutes, until the mixture is just firm in the centre when lightly pressed. Remove from the oven, leave to cool completely in the tin, then cut into 12 thin slices. This will keep in an airtight container for up to 1 week.

To serve, sprinkle the top of each posset with extra mandarin or lemon zest and serve with the shortbread alongside.

PLUM WINE JELLY WITH GINGER PLUM COMPOTE

Umeshu, plum wine, is drunk as an aperitif in Japan. The delicate sourness and sweetness of plum brings on your appetite. This dessert is one of the lightest and freshest, yet is very satisfying.

SERVES 4

For the plum wine jelly
2 teaspoon agar-agar flakes
90g sugar
180ml *umeshu* (plum wine)

For the plum compote
8 small plums, destoned and cut into quarters
3–4 tablespoons sugar
10g ginger, peeled and sliced

To serve
120ml crème fraîche, to serve
2 gingernut biscuits broken up
1 teaspoon thinly sliced lime zest or few mint leaves, to serve, optional

First, make the plum wine jelly. Put the agar-agar in a small saucepan with 300ml water and bring to the boil over high heat, stirring all the time. Turn the heat down to medium and cook for a further 2 minutes. Take off the heat, add the sugar and mix well to dissolve. Set aside to cool for about 15 minutes and then stir in the *umeshu* (plum wine) and mix.

Pour the jelly mixture into four 200ml capacity glasses to come up to one-third of each glass. Alternatively, pour the whole jelly mixture into a container. Set aside at room temperature for about 1 hour until it sets.

For the compote, in a saucepan, add the plums, sugar, ginger and 120ml water. Cut a piece of baking parchment or greaseproof paper to the size of the rim of your saucepan and place this on top of the plums, barely touching. Bring to the boil over medium heat and simmer for about 7 minutes, or until the plums are soft but still hold their shape. Once they are cooked, place in a bowl with the cooking juices and keep in the fridge until ready to eat.

To serve, take the jelly and plums out of the fridge. Spoon some of the plum compote on top of the jelly, add a dollop of crème fraîche and then crumble over the gingernut biscuits. Lastly, garnish with thinly sliced lime zest or a few mint leaves.

CARAMEL GINGER TOFU CHEESECAKE

Do you love cheesecake but hesitate because of the calories? In this version, using a proportion of tofu reduces the amount of fat intake and adds nutrients. Trust me it's tasty; I tried this dish with many anti-tofu friends, and they all loved it!

SERVES 6–8

140g gingernut biscuits
60g unsalted butter, melted
300g silken tofu
400g half or full-fat cream cheese
90g caster sugar
2 eggs, beaten
1 tablespoon calvados or brandy

For the ginger caramel sauce
60g soft dark brown sugar
20g ginger, peeled and sliced
60ml double cream

First make the caramel sauce. Put 1 tablespoon water and the brown sugar in a small saucepan and heat gently. As the sugar starts to melt, add the sliced ginger and slowly bring to the boil. Allow to simmer for 2 minutes, until all the sugar has melted and the mixture has darkened (keep an eye on it to ensure it does not burn). Pour in the double cream, little by little, mixing well all the time until the sauce becomes very thick and dark brown. Take off the heat and set aside.

Preheat the oven to 160°C/325°F/Gas Mark 3. Put the gingernut biscuits in a zip-lock plastic bag and use a rolling pin to break them up, crushing well to make fine crumbs. (Alternatively you can use a food processor to do this.) Tip the biscuit crumbs into a bowl and add the melted butter. Mix well. Tip the mixture into a 20cm springform cake tin. Use the back of a spoon to press down, packing the mixture to form an even layer about 1cm in thickness. Cover the outside base of the tin, to come to at least over halfway up the sides, with two layers of foil tightly (this will prevent leaks).

Wrap the tofu in muslin and squeeze out as much water as you can. Put the cream cheese and caster sugar in a bowl and beat well. Add the tofu, then beat again until well combined.

Slowly pour the eggs into the cheese mixture, little by little, by mixing all the time. Once completely combined, stir in the calvados or brandy.

Pour the mixture over the biscuit base in the baking tin. Smooth out the surface and get rid of any air bubbles by giving the tin a firm tap.

Place the cake tin in a large roasting tin and pour in enough just-boiled water to come halfway up the sides of the cake tin. Bake for about 10 minutes and then take it out. Pour the caramel sauce over the top, covering the entire surface. Return to the oven and continue to bake for a further 25–30 minutes, until slightly firm but still wobbly at the centre. If the water in the roasting tin gets low during cooking, top it up from time to time with freshly boiled hot water.

Once the cheesecake is cooked, remove from the oven and take the cake out of the water bath. Allow to cool in the tin until it comes to room temperature. Cover the surface with cling film and keep it in the fridge for at least 4–5 hours to set. Slice up and serve with fruit of your choice.

BUCKWHEAT CRÊPES WITH MISO CUSTARD

It's always a challenge to create an altogether slimming dessert but you can always opt for healthier ingredients, as I've done here. Buckwheat flour is much healthier than white flour. The nutty buckwheat-flour-based crêpe and salty miso custard makes a great flavour combination. You may use any fresh fruit, though figs do add a fabulous texture.

MAKES 8 PANCAKES

100g buckwheat flour
1 tablespoon caster sugar
240ml full fat milk
2 small eggs
70g unsalted butter, melted
¼ teaspoon salt
2 tablespoons vegetable or sunflower
    oil, for frying
4 fresh figs, quartered

For the miso custard
200ml full-fat milk
4 egg yolks
70g sugar
1 tablespoon miso paste

To make the crêpe mixture, put the flour and sugar in a bowl and whisk together. In a separate bowl, mix the milk and eggs until smooth.

Slowly pour the milk and egg mixture into the bowl with the flour and sugar, whisking all the time to ensure there are no lumps. Once completely mixed, pour in the melted butter and stir to combine. Cover with cling film and allow to sit for 1 hour at room temperature.

Meanwhile, make the miso custard. Heat the milk in a saucepan and bring to the boil. Put the egg yolks in a bowl with the sugar and whisk until it becomes paler in colour. Add the miso paste and whisk together until the miso has completely dissolved.

Pour half the hot milk over the egg and sugar mixture, stir well, then pour through a sieve back into the pan. Place over medium heat, stirring all the time until the mixture thickens to the consistency of double cream. If the consistency is too thick, add a dash of milk. Take off the heat and keep warm.

Heat a frying pan over medium heat. Soak kitchen paper in a little vegetable oil and carefully wipe the pan to grease it. Add a small ladleful of the batter, tilting the pan slightly to make a thin crêpe. Cook for 1 minute until the edges start to come away from the pan, then turn the crêpe over carefully to cook the other side for a further 1 minute. Remove from the pan and repeat the process until all the batter is finished. As you cook them, keep the pancakes piled up on one large plate, laying kitchen paper between each one so they don't stick together. Do not put in the oven as they will overcook and dry out.

If you have a blowtorch, quickly char the cut sides of the figs. (Fresh figs are perfectly nice but charring them a little adds a nice caramelised flavour.)

To serve, roll up the crêpe and pour the warm miso custard over the top. Place the figs to the side and enjoy.

YUZU GINGER SORBET

Yuzu and ginger are often used in Japanese cooking to add punchy flavour. The tanginess of yuzu and freshness of ginger makes this one of the most refreshing desserts.

SERVES 4

500ml white wine
120g caster sugar
2 tablespoons liquid glucose
100ml yuzu juice
50g ginger, peeled

In a saucepan, bring the wine and 500ml water to the boil over medium-high heat. Stir in the sugar and cook over medium heat, for about 20 minutes, until reduced to a syrupy consistency. Once the quantity has reduced by 40–50 per cent, turn off the heat.

Add the glucose and yuzu juice, and whisk together well to get rid of any lumps of glucose.

Grate the ginger, place in a small sieve and use the back of a spoon to squeeze out the ginger juices into the syrup. Mix well.

Place the pan in a sink of cold water and let it cool to room temperature. Transfer to the freezer to chill completely. Then pour the chilled sorbet mixture into an ice cream maker and churn until frozen (according to the manufacturer's instructions). Alternatively, pour the chilled sorbet mixture into a shallow, freezer-proof container, cover with a lid and freeze until firm, whisking the mixture 3 or 4 times (every hour or so) to break up the ice crystals during freezing.

BLACK SESAME PRALINE ICE CREAM

The nuttiness and slight bitter taste of the black sesame seeds makes a particularly tasty dessert that has an unusual but appealing colour, too.

SERVES 4

350ml double cream
350ml soy milk or semi-skimmed milk
2 egg yolks, plus 1 whole egg
80g caster sugar
4 gingernut biscuits, to serve, optional

For the black sesame praline
170g caster sugar
50g black sesame seeds

To make the sesame praline, put the sugar in a heavy-based saucepan and set over low heat. Allow the sugar to gradually melt, slightly tilting the pan but do not stir or mix. When the last bit of sugar is just about to melt, add 1 teaspoon water and tilt the pan using a circular motion. Tip in the sesame seeds and shake the pan a little, making sure all the sesame seeds are well coated in the caramel (do not taste this as it is extremely hot). Tip the caramel onto a wide sheet of foil or baking parchment and use a spatula to quickly spread it out. Allow to cool and harden for 15 minutes, then carefully peel it off the foil or parchment.

Heat the cream and milk in a saucepan until hot but not boiling. Meanwhile, whisk the egg yolks and whole egg with the sugar in a large bowl. Very slowly pour in the hot cream and milk mixture, whisking vigorously to combine.

Return the mixture back to the pan and bring to a simmer over very low heat for 5 minutes, stirring all the time with a wooden spoon until the mixture thickens to the consistency of custard. Be very careful not to overcook the mixture, or have the heat too high, otherwise the eggs will scramble. Remove from the heat and set aside to cool to room temperature.

Meanwhile, break up the sesame praline into small pieces, then crush using a mortar and pestle or food processor to make fine crumbs. Stir the praline crumbs through the cooled custard and transfer to the fridge for 1 hour.

Transfer the chilled custard into an ice cream maker and churn until frozen (according to the manufacturer's instructions). Alternatively, pour the chilled custard into a shallow, freezer-proof container, cover with a lid and freeze until firm, whisking the mixture 3 or 4 times (every hour or so) to break up the ice crystals during freezing.

Allow the ice cream to soften slightly at room temperature or in the fridge before scooping into bowls and serving with gingernut biscuits if you like.

CHERRY BLOSSOM ICE CREAM

For me, cherry blossoms are the ultimate representation of Japan. In this recipe, the saltiness of the preserved flowers is an exciting and unique addition to this pretty ice cream. Salted cherry blossoms are hard to find in shops but they can be found online. I encourage you to make your own; it takes time but it is definitely worth it.

MAKES ABOUT 1 LITRE

350ml double cream
350ml soy milk
2 egg yolks, plus 1 whole egg
70g caster sugar
60g cherry jam

For the salted cherry blossoms
100–120g cherry blossoms
10 tablespoons salt
3 tablespoons plum vinegar

When picking the cherry blossoms, pick ones that are 60–80 per cent open. If they are fully open, the petals will fall off too easily. Put the cherry blossoms in a large bowl and gently rinse with cold water taking care not to tear the blossoms. Drain and then gently pat the blossoms dry with kitchen paper.

Arrange the cherry blossoms in a container and sprinkle all over with 2 tablespoons salt, making sure to coat them well. Find 2 identical large bowls and place all the blossoms in one and then fill the other bowl with water. Place the bowl with the water on top of the bowl with the blossoms – this will press them down evenly. Allow to sit in a cool place for 2 days.

Remove the bowl of water and take out the blossoms. Squeeze any excess moisture from the blossoms and lay them, in a single layer, in a shallow container. Pour over the plum vinegar, cover and allow to marinate for 3–5 days. Then, squeeze the vinegar out.

Arrange the blossoms on a flat bamboo colander (or colander) and allow them to air-dry for 24–48 hours in a shaded place. The outer petals should be dry but the inner ones may still be a little damp, which is perfectly fine.

Put the blossoms in an airtight jar then pack with the remaining salt (you may need more salt depending on jar size). Make sure all the blossoms are buried in salt. This will keep for up to a year stored in a cool, dark place.

When you are ready to make the ice cream, briefly rinse 60g of salted cherry blossoms and lightly squeeze out any excess water (keep the remainder for another time). Put them in a food processor or coffee/spice grinder and blitz until you have almost a fine powder. Set aside.

Heat the cream and soy milk in a saucepan over medium heat until hot but not boiling.

Recipe continued on page 228

Whilst the cream and milk are heating up, whisk the egg yolks and egg, sugar and cherry jam in a large bowl. Very slowly pour half of the hot cream and milk mixture into the egg mixture, whisking vigorously.

Pour the mixture back into the pan and place over medium-low heat. Bring to a simmer, stirring all the time with a wooden spoon, until the mixture becomes a custard consistency. Remove from the heat.

Stir the salted cherry blossoms into the custard mixture and then let it cool to room temperature before transferring to the fridge for 2 hours or freezer for about 30 minutes.

Transfer the chilled custard into an ice cream maker and churn until frozen (according to the manufacturer's instructions). Alternatively, pour the chilled custard into a shallow, freezer-proof container, cover with a lid and freeze until firm, whisking the mixture 3 or 4 times (every hour or so) to break up the ice crystals during freezing.

SHO-YU ICE CREAM MARBLED WITH CHOCOLATE

Sho-yu, aka soy sauce, is the most important seasoning in Japanese savoury cooking. It has been somewhat overlooked when it comes to sweet dishes. But why not? Give it a try, I promise it works. The chocolate marbling provides a delectable dimension to this ice cream. For this ice cream, you'll need an ice cream maker for the best results.

MAKES 1 LITRE

4 egg yolks
80g caster sugar
300ml milk or soy milk
200ml double cream
3 tablespoons tamari soy sauce
   (*sho-yu*)

For the chocolate sauce
50g dark chocolate (minimum 70 per
   cent cocoa solids)
1 tablespoon glucose
125ml double cream
1 tablespoon sugar

To make the ice cream, whisk the egg yolks and caster sugar together in a bowl until pale and thickened.

Pour the milk and cream into a saucepan and bring up to the boil. Turn off the heat and the pour half of the hot milk and cream mixture into the eggs and whisk together well.

Pour the mixture back into the pan along with the remaining milk and cream. Heat gently, stirring all the time with a wooden spoon, until the mixture thickens slightly.

Add the soy sauce; this will slightly loosen the custard. Simmer for a further 1 minute, stirring all the time, until the texture thickens to a custard but don't let it boil. Turn off the heat and allow to cool to room temperature.

Once the mixture has cooled, chill in the fridge for at least 1 hour.

Meanwhile, make the chocolate sauce. Break the chocolate into small pieces and put in a heatproof bowl set over a pan of simmering water. Gently allow to melt until completely smooth. Take the melted chocolate off the heat and add the remaining ingredients, mixing well. Allow to cool.

Transfer the chilled custard into an ice cream maker and churn until frozen (according to the manufacturer's instructions). Pour a thin layer of the ice cream into a wide plastic container and drizzle over the chocolate sauce randomly. Top with another layer of ice cream and repeat to create the marbled effect. Put the lid on and freeze until firm.

Note: Feel free to use good-quality shop-bought chocolate sauce.

INDEX

INDEX

A

adzuki beans 18
    paste 214
Agedashi Tofu in Prawn Broth 170
alcohol 25
apples: miso pork belly 119
Arame Seaweed and Calamari Salad 154
Asian Tofu Dango Soup 168
Asparagus and Umami Dashi Jelly with Onsen Tamago 141
aubergine:
    baked with miso, chicken and mozzarella 152
    steak with smoked tofu and shiitake mushrooms 174
Autumn Rice 64
avocado:
    crisp-fried with shiso 47
    dulse seaweed salad 157
    and eel roll 197
    mousse with tuna tataki 100

B

Baked Aubergine with Miso, Chicken and Mozzarella 152
bamboo shoot 22
Bang Bang Chicken with Somen Noodles 79
beef:
    cubes with Japanese tomato sauce 125
    shabu shabu nabe 186
    wafu steak 122
Black Sesame and Cherry Blossom Tortes 213
Black Sesame Praline Ice Cream 226
Blowtorched Pickled Mackerel 94
Blowtorched Salmon with Yuzu Ponzo Dressing 103
bonito flakes 18
broccoli: pesto with soba noodles 89
Buckwheat Crêpes with Miso Custard 223
Butternut Squash with Okra and Almond 142

C

cakes: black sesame and cherry blossom tortes 213
calamari:
    and arame seaweed salad 154
    with pork, green beans and soy-mayo 120
    stuffed with rice 60
    tempura with watercress 40
Caramel Ginger Tofu Cheesecake 222
Chakin Tofu in Ginger Broth 163
cherry blossom:
    ice cream 227
    tortes with black sesame 213
chicken:
    aubergine with miso and mozzarella 152
    bang bang with somen noodles 79
    breast with yakumi sauce 135
    hot and sour broth 131
    and prawn quenelles with miso soup 109
    tofu fritters with prawn 164
    and vegetable katsu 132
Chinese cabbage 22
chocolate sauce 229
chrysanthemum leaves 22
Cloudy Soup 145
courgettes:
    nigiri 206
    pickled and samphire 148
crab:
    and prawn cakes 107
    tempura roll 201
Crisp-Fried Shiso Avocado 47
Crispy Prawn Wontons 39
Cucumber and Wakame Gunkan Nigiri 207
curries: udon with curry sauce 80

D

daikon radish 22
desserts 209
    buckwheat crêpes with miso custard 223
    caramel ginger tofu cheesecake 222
    green tea dorayaki pancakes 214
    matcha soufflé 217
    plum wine jelly with ginger plum compote 221
    yuzu posset with sesame shortbread 218
    see also ice cream; sorbets
dips: edamame and tofu 49
duck:
    with plum miso 129
    seared with soba in broth 76

Dulse Seaweed and Avocado Salad
    with Ume Dressing 157

E

edamame beans 23
    dip with tofu 49
    with miso scallop 113
eel:
    and avocado roll 197
    donburi 59
eggs 159
    Japanese sweet omelette 177
    onsen tamago with asparagus 141
    savoury steamed custard 176
    vegetable tamago-yaki with
        ponzu sauce 179
    yakisoba with fried egg 87

F

fish 93
    monkfish nabe 189
    sardines with umeboshi 97
    sea bass with yuzu miso 106
    sea bream with yuzu ponzo jelly
        104
    yellow tail sashimi with yuzu and
        truffle dressing 98
    see also eel; mackerel; salmon;
        seafood; tuna
fruit:
    apple with pork belly 119
    strawberry mochi 210

see also plums; yuzu

G

ginger 22
    broth with tofu 163
    meatballs 116
    miso pea patties 37
    plum pork in lettuce cups 38
green beans: with pork and calamari
    120
Green Tea Dorayaki Pancakes 214
Grilled Duck with Plum Miso on
    Magnolia Leaves 129
Grilled Salmon and Rice Soup 52
Guineafowl with Miso Sweetcorn
    Purée 130
gyoza dumplings 138

H

Horse Mackerel and Onion Patties 43
hotpots see nabe

I

ice cream:
    black sesame praline 226
    cherry blossom 227
    sho-yu with chocolate 229

J

Japanese Miso Risotto 68
Japanese Padron Peppers 48
Japanese Pot-Au-Feu 191
Japanese Savoury Pancake 84
Japanese-style Lobster Thermidor
    110
Japanese Sweet Omelette 177

K

Kombu-cured Sea Bream with Yuzu
    Ponzo Jelly 104

L

lobster: Japanese-style Thermidor
    110
lotus root 22
    salad 151

M

mackerel:
    horse mackerel and onion patties
        43
    pickled 94
matcha 25
    pancakes 214
    soufflé 217

mayonnaise 18, 31
    spicy soy 120
    wasabi 47, 55
meat 115
    sweet ginger meatballs 116
    teriyaki croquettes 121
    veal fillet with ginger, soy and
        blue cheese sauce 126
    venison tataki with parsnip mash
        34
    see also beef; pork; poultry
mirin 19
miso 19
    apple pork belly 119
    arancini 44
    ginger pea patties 37
    risotto 68
    scallop with edamame purée 113
    wafu steak 122
    white spaghetti carbonara 90
mochi (rice cakes) 19
    rainbow veg with kombu butter
        sauce 144
    strawberry 210
Monkfish Nabe 189
mushrooms 23
    with aubergine and smoked tofu
        174
    Autumn Rice 64
    with steamed tofu and scallops
        173
    udon noodles with seaweed 87
    wild Japanese rice 56

N

nabe 181
    Japanese pot-au-feu 191
    monkfish 189
    selections 182
    shabu shabu 186
    soy milk and chilli 188
    sukiyaki 185
noodles 18, 71
    bang bang chicken with somen
        79
    broth 29
    duck breast soba in broth 76
    ramen with char-siu pork 73
    savoury pancake 84
    shirataki with chuka sauce 75
    soba rolls with nori sheet 83
    soba with broccoli pesto 89
    udon with curry sauce 80
    udon with mushrooms and
        seaweed 87
    white miso spaghetti carbonara
        90
    yakisoba with fried egg 86

O

onions: deep-fried 79

P

pancakes:
    buckwheat crêpes with miso
        custard 223
    green tea dorayaki 214
    Japanese savoury 84
parsnips: mash with venison tataki
    34
pasta: white miso spaghetti carbonara
    90
patties:
    mackerel and onion 43
    miso ginger pea 37
peas: miso ginger patties 37
peppers: Japanese padron 48
Pickled Courgette and Samphire 148
plums:
    and ginger pork in lettuce cups
        38
    miso with duck 129
    wine jelly with ginger plum
        compote 221
pork:
    with calamari, green beans and
        soy-mayo 120
    char-siu with ramen noodles 73
    miso apple pork belly 119
    plum and ginger in lettuce cups
        38
    with steamed tofu 160
poultry 115
    guineafowl with sweetcorn purée
        130
    see also chicken; duck
prawns:
    broth with tofu 170
    and chicken quenelles with miso
        soup 109

and crab cakes 107
crispy wantons 39
tofu fritters with chicken 164
and tofu on rice 63
pumpkin 22

R

Ramen Noodles with Pork Broth and
    Char-Siu Park 73
rice 18, 51
    autumn 65
    brown 18
    calamari stuffed 60
    eel donburi 59
    hijiki seaweed 67
    miso arancini 44
    miso risotto 68
    plain 29
    prawn and tofu 62
    soup with salmon 52
    sushi 30
    tuna tartare 55
    vegan donburi 69
    wild mushroom 56
    see also mochi (rice cakes)
rice vinegar 18
rice wine 18
Rich Vegetarian Roll 202

S

sake 18, 25
salads:
    arame seaweed and calamari 154
    dulse seaweed and avocado 157
    lotus root 151
salmon:
    inside out roll 198
    scattered sushi – chirashi 194
    soup with rice 52
    winter soup 101
    with yuzu ponzo dressing 103
sansho pepper 18
Sardines with Umeboshi 97
sauces:
    chocolate 229
    chuka 75
    ginger, soy and blue cheese 126
    Japanese tomato 125
    oroshi teriyaki 167
    ponzo 40, 179
    sesame 79
    teriyaki 31
    tonkatsu 84
    yakumi 135
    yuzu miso 106
    see also mayonnaise
Savoury Steamed Egg Custard 176
scallops:
    with edamame purée 113
    with steamed tofu and
        mushrooms 173
Sea Bass with Yuzu Miso 106
sea bream: with yuzu ponzo jelly 104
seafood 93
    lobster thermidor 110
    see also calamari; crab; prawns;
        scallops

Seared Duck Breast Soba in Broth 76
seaweed 19, 137
    arame and calamari salad 154
    dulse and avocado salad 157
    hijiki rice 67
    powder 18
    toasted 19
    udon noodles with mushrooms
        87
Sesame Lotus Root Salad 151
sesame oil 18
sesame seeds 19
    black sesame and cherry blossom
        tortes 213
    black sesame praline ice cream
        226
seven-spice powder 19
Shabu Shabu Nabe 186
shallots: deep-fried 79
shiitake mushrooms:
    with aubergine and smoked tofu
        174
    with steamed tofu and scallops
        173
Shirataki Noodles with Chuka Sauce
    75
shiso 22
    crisp-fried avocado 47
Sho-Yu Ice Cream Marbled with
    Chocolate 229
Soba Noodle Rolls with Nori Sheet
    83
Soba Noodles with Broccoli Pesto 89
Soft Prawn and Crab Cakes 107
Soft-Shell Crab Roll 201
sorbets: yuzu ginger 225
soups:
    Asian tofu dango 168

chicken in hot and sour broth
131
cloudy 145
miso with prawn and chicken
quenelles 109
noodle broth 29
salmon and rice 52
salmon winter 101
tofu in ginger broth 163
tofu in prawn broth 170
tomato with tofu croutons 147
Soy Milk and Chilli Nabe 188
soy sauce 19
ice cream with chocolate 229
soybeans 23
Spicy Miso Soup with Prawn and
Chicken Quenelles 109
spinach 22
spring onions 22
squid *see calamari*
Steamed Tofu with Scallops and
Shiitake Mushrooms 173
Steamed Tofu with Spicy Pork 160
stews *see nabe*
stock:
dashi 19, 28
vegetarian 28
Strawberry Mochi 210
Sukiyaki Nabe 185
Super Vegan Donburi 69
sushi 193
crab roll 201
eel and avocado roll 197
hand-moulded nigiri 206
rice 30
salmon inside out roll 198
salmon scattered – chirashi 194
vegetarian roll 202
sushi vinegar 19

Sweet Ginger Meatballs 116
sweet potato 22
sweetcorn:
nigiri 207
purée with guineafowl 130

tea 25; *see also* matcha
tempura:
calamari and watercress 40
crab 201
vegetable 153
Teriyaki Croquettes 121
teriyaki sauce 31
tofu 23, 159
Asian dango soup 168
burgers with oroshi teriyaki sauce
167
caramel ginger cheesecake 222
dip with edamame 49
fritters with prawn and chicken
164
in ginger broth 163
in prawn broth 170
and prawns on rice 63
sesame katsu 169
smoked with aubergine and
mushrooms 174
steamed with scallops and
shiitake mushroom 173
steamed with spicy pork 160
tomatoes:
Japanese sauce 125
soup with tofu croutons 147

tuna:
tartare rice 55
tataki with avocado mousse 100

U

Udon Noodles with Curry Sauce 80
Udon Noodles with Enoki
Mushrooms and Arame Seaweed
87
Umami Tomato Soup with Tofu
Croutons 147
Unagi Eel Donburi 59

V

Veal Fillet with Ginger, Soy and Blue
Cheese Sauce 126
vegetables 137
asparagus with dashi jelly and
egg 141
broccoli pesto with soba noodles
89
butternut squash with okra and
almond 142
Chinese cabbage 22
cloudy soup 145
deep-fried onions (shallots) 79
gyoza dumplings 138
hand-moulded nigiri 206
lotus root salad 151
miso ginger pea patties 37
padron peppers 48

parsnip mash with venison tataki 34

pumpkin 22

rainbow veg with mochi and butter sauce 144

rich vegetarian roll 202

spinach 22

spring onions 22

sweet potato 22

tamago-yaki with thick ponzo sauce 179

tempura 153

see also aubergine; courgettes; mushrooms; sweetcorn

Vegetarian Gyoza Dumplings 138

Venison Tataki with Wasabi Parsnip Mash 34

Y

Yakisoba with Fried Egg 86

Yellow Tail Sashimi with Yuzu and Truffle Dressing 98

yuzu 23

ginger sorbet 225

posset with sesame shortbread 218

W

Wafu Miso Steak 122

wasabi (Japanese horseradish) 18

parsnip mash 34

White Miso Spaghetti Carbonara 90

Wild Japanese Mushroom Rice 56

ACKNOWLEDGEMENTS

I'm thrilled to publish my second book which showcases contemporary Japanese food with a fusion twist. I was very lucky to have such a fantastic team to help me to create this book.

I'd like to dedicate my greatest thanks to my parents and brother in Kyoto, Japan. Despite the distance and only meeting once a year for our annual get together, they are always supporting me emotionally. Without my strong family tie in Kyoto, I could not be successfully doing what I do.

Tom and Jack, my precious sons who have always given me the courage and strength to take on the challenge of new projects. They are now grown up and independent but still the most important people for me to please and spoil with my cooking. I'm so glad that they have each grown to become 'foodies' who appreciate good food and good chefs.

I'd also like to thank my talented photographer Jodi, my hard working home economist Elaine for testing my recipes and my smart writer and PR assistant Chloe who undertook research for this book. This book would not have come together without them all.

Last but not least, I have to thank my publisher Absolute Press, an imprint of Bloomsbury Publishing PLC, for taking on another adventure with me in publishing my second Japanese cookbook and providing an excellent team to work with. Huge thanks to Jon Croft and the Absolute team for making the second book come to be.

ABOUT THE AUTHOR

Reiko Hashimoto was born in the ancient capital of Japan, Kyoto, and grew up with a food fanatic mother who continues to influence Reiko's love for traditional Japanese flavours today. After studying English Literature at university, Reiko travelled the world for work, picking up fusion dishes and nurturing her understanding of food from all over the world. With this knowledge, Reiko decided to make a career from cooking and teaching and set up her business, Hashi Cooking, in London.

That was 14 years ago; in this time Reiko has taught thousands of students to create delicious and authentic Japanese dishes, from scratch, in a Western kitchen. While Reiko has taught chefs of Le Cordon Bleu, many students are complete beginners, which means Reiko's recipes are accessible and easy to follow – debunking the myth that Japanese cookery is complicated.

Through her school, Reiko has developed a close following and now also teaches in catering schools, restaurants, exclusive members clubs and luxury hotels worldwide. Meanwhile, Reiko has appeared on television programmes such as *Good Food Live* and *The Great British Kitchen* as a guest chef, and has been named a finalist in the 'People's Choice' category of the British Cookery School Awards.

In 2011, Reiko took her passion for teaching a step further, producing her first cookery book, *Hashi: A Japanese Cookery Course*, a definitive book on how to cook Japanese food at home. This second book focuses on another aspect of life that is incredibly important to Reiko, health and wellbeing, all through beautifully presented and – most significantly – delicious dishes.

As Reiko often says, 'it must always be tasty!'

Publisher: Jon Croft
Commissioning Editor: Meg Avent
Art Director and Designer: Kim Musgrove
Project Editor: Emily North
Photographer: Jodi Hinds, www.jodihinds.com
Photographer's Assistants: Tristan Fennell & Pablo Antolí
Crockery for photography: Courtesy of Doki Japanese
Tableware, www.dokiltd.co.uk
Calligraphy: Reiko Hashimoto
Researcher: Chloe Hodge
Copyeditor: Kate Wanwimolruk
Home Economist: Elaine Byfield
Proofreader: Zoe Ross
Indexer: Zoe Ross